Marquart's Works

VOLUME
V

CHRISTENDOM

Edited by
Herman J. Otten

LUTHERAN NEWS, INC., New Haven, Missouri

Marquart's Works

Library of Congress Card
Lutheran News, Inc.
684 Luther Lane
New Haven, MO 63068
Published 2014
Printed in the United States of America
Lightning Source, Inc., La Vergne, TN
ISBN #978-0-9832409-1-4

TABLE OF CONTENTS

FOREWORD

Dr. Marquart was a beloved Professor by all the students that sat in his classes. His ability to simplify great theological concepts made him a favorite Teacher for all the students who attended the Seminary. He not only instilled in us a love for Theology, but he also showed us how it was to be applied in a pastor's daily calling.

However, these writings are not just for pastors. Even dedicated laymen will be able to grasp and learn from this great Teacher of the Church. Whenever and wherever Dr. Marquart made a presentation, you would soon see that he was eagerly sought out, not just by pastors but also by laymen. They too recognized his genius in refuting those who denied the Word of God. He was as popular with laymen as he was with pastors. Here in these volumes you will once again be able to take your place and listen to this great Teacher, as he clearly enunciates various topics from a thoroughly Lutheran perspective. Since these multiple volumes consist of the various topics that Dr. Marquart addressed over his illustrious life, you will find it hard to put these volumes down.

Having Dr. Marquart's writings in book form will once again allow this fearless Champion of the Church to speak to the issues that continue to plague the Church from one generation to the next. False doctrine continues to be rehashed and sent out with new clothes. As the Proverb goes, "there is nothing new under the sun." Dr. Marquart had the remarkable ability to dissect what the issue was, and why it was, and still is, false doctrine. Confessional Lutherans from all over the world were always eager to attend Dr. Marquart's lectures. They recognized that he was a giant among men. Anyone concerned about the welfare of the Church will want to have these volumes on their bookshelf.

It appears that the Almighty Savior of the Church, in His infinite wisdom, chooses to send out only a few Teachers of the Church. One may make a very short list of these esteemed gifts from God. Luther, Chemnitz, Gerhard, Walther, Pieper, Preus, and Marquart. Their writings stand the test of time. These men did not write for some passing fad, that is here today and then blown away by tomorrow's changing wind vane. Any pastor or layman, who has a desire and love for the Truth, will not be disappointed with these volumes. Every congregation that has a love for the Lord and His saving Gospel, would do well to purchase the writings from these Teachers of the Church. God had His good reasons for raising these men up and sending them out, and it would be wise for pastors and laymen to read, mark, learn and inwardly digest the writings of these great defenders of the Gospel.

Rev. Herman Otten is to be commended for publishing the writings of Dr. Kurt Marquart. This may well be Rev. Otten's finest and most enduring contribution to the Church.

Rev. Ray R. Ohlendorf
Salem Lutheran Church
Taylorsville, NC
4th Sunday in Lent 2014

i

Acknowledgements

Well Herman,

As usual you find yourself doing what unsere beliebte Synode should have done long ago. The fact that CPH has not already published a book of Kurt's writings is an absolute travesty. It is an indictment of the politics before theology which has destroyed the orthodoxy of the LCMS. Our Savior Lutheran Church will stand by you in the worthy project. Back in the dark days when Bohlmann and his supporters were after Robert Preus we published a number of Kurt's magnificent essays on Robert's behalf. Modern Missouri has never produced another theologian comparable to him either in confessional fidelity or eloquence. We are proud and eager to take part in this belated effort. "Gottes Wort Und Luthers Lehr Vergehet Nun Und Nimmermehr."

Larry White, Pastor
Our Saviour Lutheran Church
Houston, Texas

Thanks to Luke Otten for arranging the publication of these volumes and to Naomi Finck, Natalie Hoerstkamp, for type-setting.

Thanks to Grace Otten for recognizing the importance of publishing *Marquart's Works* ever since they first began appearing in *Christian News* more than 50 years ago. Thanks to Scott Meyer, "America's confessional Lutheran" lay historian and President of the Concordia Historical Institute whose appreciation of Marquart's works and encouragement helped make the publication of these volumes possible.

PREFACE

Dr. C. F. W. Walther, first president of The Lutheran Church-Missouri Synod, has been rightly referred to as "The American Luther." As the editor of a Christian weekly for 51 years, the undersigned has reviewed thousands of books. During all these years he has published the writings of many theologians. The index at the back of Volume V of the *Christian News Encyclopedia* lists the names of hundreds of theologians whose writings have appeared in *Christian News*. Some, like Kurt Marquart, were also good friends. Yet, the editor knows of no theologian who deserves the title "The International Lutheran" more than Kurt Marquart. The editor's wife, Grace, is a graduate of Concordia College, St. Paul Minnesota and Valparaiso University. There she studied under some prominent theologians who later became professors at Concordia Seminary, St. Louis and Seminex. In 1963 Grace Otten and Kurt Marquart were *CN*'s reporters at the Fourth Assembly of the Lutheran World Federation in Helsinki, Finland. Following the LWF Assembly she and the editor's brother, Walter, who knew Marquart for 54 years, accompanied him on a twenty city lecture tour in the U.S. Grace shares the editor's evaluation of Kurt Marquart. She helped make it possible together with Luke Otten, Ruth Rethemeyer, Mary Beth Otten, Kristina Bailey and the Missourian Publishing Company, Washington, Missouri, to get *Marquart's Legacy* published in 2006 not long after his death. The 76 page *Marquart's Legacy* is available from *Christian News* for $5.00. It includes photos of Marquart and family and information about two professionally made videos showing Marquart in action.

Marquart's Legacy begins with a brief biography of Kurt Marquart. Then follows "Remembrances of a Former Seminary Roommate," the editor of *Christian News*. Next comes "The Lasting Legacy of Kurt Marquart" as expressed by many who knew him well.

The appendixes list the writings and reports of Kurt Marquart which have appeared in 44 volumes of *Christian News* (1962-2006), *A Christian Handbook on Vital Issues*, the five volumes of the *Christian News Encyclopedia*, *Luther Today, What Would He Do or Say?* and *Crisis in Christendom-Seminex Ablaze*. The lasting legacy of a great theologian and genius like Kurt Marquart can best be found in his works. *CN* suggested in 2006 that the Lutheran Church-Missouri Synod's Concordia Publishing House should publish *Marquart's Works*.

The questions at the end of each section are included to make *Marquart's Works* helpful for study. In an age when faith in historic Christianity is declining in all of the major denominations, *Marquart's Works* can be used to encourage and strengthen faithful Christians and begin a 21st Century Reformation and 21st Century Formula of Concord by the 500th anniversary of the Reformation in 2017.

Herman Otten
Reformation, 2014

A SPECIFICATION OF
A DOCTRINAL ISSUES

(This 1959 document is in "Concordia Seminary, St. Louis vs. Otten Case – Book of Documentation Arranged by Kurt Marquart")

This statement is not a list of charges, but a presentation, side by side, of (A) Synod's historic position as I have learned it from the Catechism and other authoritative sources, and (B) positions of St. Louis Professors, defended publicly in class and in some cases elaborated in discussions with me.

In listing the two sets of positions I am not asserting irreconcilable conflict. A thorough, incisive examination, which I as a student was of course in no position to carry out, may reveal some apparent differences to be merely matters of terminology or emphasis. My listing of the two sets of positions is not a charge of false doctrine, but an allegation that such and such positions are being held and taught. All I am stating is the need to clarify scrupulously the relation between the old *modus docendi* and the new.

I. De Scriptura

Position A
1. Holy Scripture is the verbally inspired written Word of God. (*Brief Statement.* #1)

2. Scripture is the inspired Word of God and the only infallible rule of faith and practice." (*Mutual Responsibility*, A)

3. Therefore the Holy Scriptures "contain no errors or contradictions, but . . . are in all their parts and words the infallible truth, also in those parts which treat of historical, and other secular matters." (*Brief Statement.* #1)

4. "We reject the doctrine . . . that Holy Scripture . . . does, or at least might contain error." (*Brief Statement* #5) "Whether a person takes the Christian attitude toward Scripture and lets Scripture be the Word of God, is seen at once from the attitude he takes as to the possibility of error in Scriptures." (Pieper 1, p. 280)

5. "It is absolutely necessary that we maintain the doctrine of inspiration as taught by our orthodox dogmaticians. If the possibility that Scripture contained the least error were admitted, it would become the business of *man* to sift the truth from the error. . . . The least deviation from the old inspiration doctrine introduces a rationalistic germ into theology and infects the whole body of doctrine." (Quoted in *Walther and the Church*, p. 14)

Positon B
1. Holy Scripture is the verbally inspired written Word of God.[a]
2. Scripture is "the inspired Word, of God and the only infallible[b] rule

of faith and practice." (*Mutual Responsibility*, A)

3. But Scripture contains errors and contradictions.

4. We cannot *a priori*, dogmatically deny the possibility of errors. Inerrancy is an open question.

5. The old dogmaticians, also Pieper and Engelder, took extremist positions on inspiration and inerrancy.

Notes:

a) Since those who deny the inerrancy and plenary inspiration freely subscribe to "verbal inspiration" (Cf. Appeal. Appendix C, 49, 2 and Exhibit G, pp. 1 and 2), the term "verbal inspiration" by itself is meaningless.

b) Expressions like the U.L.C.A.'s "the inspired Word of God . . . the only infallible rule and standard of faith and practice" (Constitution, Art. II, sec. 1) do not confess the inerrancy, nor touch the real issue, for at the same time the U.L.C.A. declares through its commissioners: "Our commissioners were unable to accept the statement of the Missouri Synod that the Scriptures are the infallible truth 'also in those parts which treat of historical geographical, and other secular matters.' We find the words quoted not in accordance with our Lutheran Confessions...nor with the Scriptures themselves." (C.T.M., Vol. X, Jan. 1939, no. 1, p. 65)

II. De Satisfactione Christi

Position A

1. The *vicarious satisfaction* means that Christ has, as a Substitute of mankind, fully increased God's wrath for sin and satisfied the demands of His justice. (Pieper, II,344ff)

2. "Vicarious satisfaction" is not a "picture" but a literal reality. "Not merely the 'basic idea,' as the moderns say, is correct, but the whole matter is entirely Scriptural." (Pieper, II, 347)

3. "'A change of attitude *on the part of God* is meant.' . . . a change took place, not in men, but in God." (Pieper, II, 346)

4. "In lucid and exact language the Formula of Concord teaches that the *obedienta Christi activa* is an integral part of His substitutional satisfaction . . . Restricting the *obedienta activa* to the 'willing assumption of suffering' is here expressly rejected." (Pieper, II, 374)

Position B

1. One should hesitate to affirm that God's wrath was appeased, since He still has wrath over sin.

2. The "vicarious satisfaction" is one of the Biblical pictures of the Atonement.

3. Since God is immutable, there cannot be a change in the mind of God.

4. The theory of Christ's active obedience has no Scriptural support, the usual passages being inapplicable.

5. We do not know to whom the Ransom of Matt. 20:28 was paid, since Scripture does not specify this.

III. De Ecclesia

Position A

1. The Church consists of all those and only of those who have saving faith. (*Brief Statement*, #24)

2. An isolated believer (e.g., one on a desert island) is just as much in the Church as any other believer, namely solely and alone by virtue of his faith.

3. Hypocrites and other unbelievers are in no sense members of the Body of Christ (i.e. the Church, properly speaking) though they are mixed with the Church in external Christendom, which, however is not the *corpus Christi* but a *corpus mixtum*. (*Kirche und Amt*, Thesis 2)

4. The Church *qua* Church, i.e. "the Church, in the proper sense of the term, is invisible." (*Kirche und Amt*, Thesis 3)

5. The Church is not a Platonic dream..., but a concrete reality.

Position B

1. The Church consists of the Christians.

2. From the New Testament point of view a Christian is in the Church only when he stands in a relation of active communication with one or more other Christians.

3. Hypocrites are, in a sense, part of the Body of Christ.

4. The Church is invisible, that is, it is not an external polity, but "invisible" does not mean "cannot be seen."

5. The Church is not a Platonic dream, but a concrete reality.

IV. De Anima et de Resurrectione

Position A

1. Man is a dichotomous (or trichotomous) being consisting of a body and a spirit or soul.

2. Man's spirit or soul is immortal and survives physical death.

3. The Jehovah's Witnesses' denial of immortality is anti-scriptural.

4. The Bible teaches
    a) the immortality of the soul, and
    b) the resurrection of the body.

5. Resurrection means the reconstitution of all human corpses and the glorification of the bodies of believers on Judgment Day. (Pieper I, 475 ff; III, 507 ff)

Position B

1. Man is a psychosomatic unity.

2. The immortality of the soul is not a Christian, Biblical teaching. Hence several hymns in The Lutheran Hymnal ought to be taken out.

3. With regard to immortality, Jehovah's Witnesses are more Biblical than traditional Lutherans.

4. The Bible teaches
    a) no immortality of the soul, but only

3

b) the resurrection of the body.

5. It is doubtful what the *"body"* is. The corpse that is buried is not the body, but the mask of the body. The corpse itself is buried never to rise again.

V. De Creatione

Position A

1. God is the Creator of all things.

2. "Where Scripture speaks historically, as, for example, in Genesis 1-3, it must be understood as speaking of literal historical facts." (Synodical Conference Statement on Scripture, Proceedings, 1958, p. 44)

3. Adam and Eve were two real, historical,[a] human individuals, created directly by God. ". . . all men are Adamites, i.e. Adam is the first man and the progenitor of all mankind. This is no theological problem, but a doctrine clearly revealed in Scripture." (Pieper, 477)

4. It is anti-Scriptural and impermissible to hold that man's physical nature originated or may have originated by means of (albeit "theistic") evolution from some other species. "Evolutionism and all that is involved is thoroughly treated and refuted in Lehre und Wehre, 46, 8-239; 55, 289-550." (Pieper, I, 470, n. 5)

5. Genesis 1 and 2 contain no contradictions.

Position B

1. God is the Creator of all things.

2. A symbolical interpretation of Genesis 1-3 or even 1-11 is permissible.

3. Adam and Eve may be taken as symbols of mankind, and not necessarily as real persons.

4. The theory of evolution, viewed as God's means of creation, cannot be dogmatically denied, but should be left a permissible opinion. (Possible qualification: personally we do not believe in evolution.)

5. Genesis 1 and 2, taken literally, are contradictory.

[a] An ambiguity may arise here by virtue of the distinction between ordinary, phenomenal, "calendar" history and some sort of transcendental, noumenal "Urgeschichte." Thus, in this sense, Adam and Eve may be said to belong to "real history" (tacitly defined as Urgeschichte"), though their actual existence in the literal sense of Genesis 1-3 may be denied.

VI. De Vetere Testamento

Position A

1. Whatever the N.T. asserts about the hermeneutics or isagogics of the O.T. or any part thereof, is in principle *ipso facto* the dogmatically binding position, to the exclusion, *e limine*, of all other interpretations.

2. St. Matt. 22:41-45 and Acts 2:14,25-31 demand the affirmation, on dogmatic grounds, of the Davidic authorship of Psalms 110 and 16 respectively.

a) Neither Scripture nor Christ in His humiliation ever taught error.
b) The theory of accommodationism is to be rejected.
   (Pieper, I, 473)

3. The O.T. directly and consciously predicts a personal Messiah. Jn.12,41; Acts 2, 30-31.
4. The O.T. teaches a blissful immortality for God's believers.
   " . . . Holy Scripture . . . clearly affirms the resurrection of the body in the Old Testament." (Pieper, III, 534-535)

Position B
1. Matters of isagogics and hemeneutics cannot be settled a priori, dogmatically, from the N.T., but, since they belong to the Bible's "history-side" rather than its "faith-side" must be settled on the basis of scientific evidence.
2. St. Matt. 22:41-45 and Acts 2:4,25-31 do not demand the affirmation of the Davidic authorship of Psalms 110 and 16, because
   a) We must take seriously the Knechtsgestalt of Scripture and Christ's state of humiliation.
   b) Christ accomodated himself to rabbinical hermeneutics and to the prevailing isagogical views.
3. The O.T.. contains no rectilinear, predictive prophecies of a personal Messiah.
4. The O.T. teaches no distinction between the fates of the good and the evil after death: Both languish as shades in Sheol.

From "Theologische Hermeneutik. Leitfaden fuer Vorlesungen," CPH, 1912:
"#28. Die voellige Uebareinstimmung der Schrift mit sich selbst muss bei ihrer Auslegung in voraus feststehen und darf in keinem Falle aufgegeben werden, da bei ihrem goettlichen Urheber eine Inkonsequenz des Denkens, Wollens, und Redens, ein Selbstwiderspruch oder ein auch noch so geringer Irrtum unmoeglich ist . . . . Es ist darum falsch, wenn behauptet wird, dass ein wirklicher Widerspruch in der Schrift vorkomme oder auch nur vorkommen koenne." (p. 15)

"#34. . . . Der christliche Exeget muss darum festhalten, sowohl dass mit dem als Erfuellung der Weissagung berichteten Ereignis Gottes vorbedachter Rat und Plan hinausgegangen ist, als auch dass fuer Verstaendnis und Auslegung der Weissagung der Bericht ueber die Erfuellung entscheidend ist . . . . Bei der Auslegung eines prophetischen Spruches oder Abschnittes des Alten Testaments hat man sich danach umzusehen, ob im Neuen Testament ausgesprochenermassen ueber ein Ereignis als Erfuellung dieser Weissagung berichtet ist. Ist dies der Fall, so ist dem Exegeten die weitere Arbeit und Untersuchung gleichsam abgenommen und auch die Bedeutung einzelner Worte sichergestellt." (p. 18)

" . . . An dem richtigen Verstaendnis messianischer Weissagungen darf sich der Exeget auch dadurch nicht irremachen laasen, dass sie oft ganz unvermittelt neben zeitgeschichtlichen Reden stehen; vgl. die Umrahmung von Jes.7, 14 Micha 2,12.13 und dazu Luther XIV,1025.1026. Ebenso muss er auch hueten vor der Verkehrtheit mancher Ausleger, die gerade bei solchen Weissagungen einen zweioder mehrfachen Sinn annehmen und die direkte messianische Beziehung in Abrede stellen,"(p. 19)

From C.F.W. Walther's **Die Evangelisch-Lutherische Kirche die wahre sichtbare Kirche Gottes auf Erden**.

"Brentiu: 'Wenn Paulus diesen (18.) Psalm von Christo auslegt, so ist keine andere Auslegung, selbst nicht eines Engels anzuerkennen.'

Derselbe: 'Da wir apostolische Zeugnisse haben, welche der Grund der Kirche sind, dass dieser (2.) Psalm von Christo, dem Sohne Gottes zu verstehen sei, so ist selbst kein Engel, geschweige ein gottloser Rabbiner, der etwas anderes lehrt, su hoeren.'" (p. 78)

"Aeg. Hunnius.... 'Allerdings ist derjenige ein Ketzer, welcher einen Artikel des Glaubens leugnet; aber nicht nur dieser, sondern auch derjenige, welcher eine geschichtliche Erzaehlung des heiling Geistes leugnet.'" (p. 122)

VII. De Praedestinatione

Position A
1. Election is to be understood in the narrow sense as an election unto final salvation which always embraces the "ordo salutis."
2. The Scriptural term "elect" refers to:
    a. only those who will finally be saved;
    b. not Zeitglaeubige
    c. not all men.
3. The "elect" can fall temporarily, but God will surely restore than and bring them to final glory. (*Brief Statement* and *13 Theses* of 1881)

Position B
1. Election is to be understood in the wider sense as an election unto eternal life which believers have now by faith; but which can be lost. Any formulation needs to take seriously all warnings against a false sense of security.
2. The Scriptural term "elect" refers to:
    a. those who will finally be saved, and
    b. also "Zeitglaeubige" but
    c. not all men.

6

3. The individuals to whom the Scriptures apply the term "elect" can fall; whether permanently we know not and say not.

VIII. The Brief Statement
Position A
1. Public teachers of the Missouri Synod are sworn to the Sacred Scriptures and the Lutheran Symbols.

2. Therefore public teachers are bound to the Brief Statement as an authoritative statement, in the face of contradictory interpretations, of how the Missouri Synod understands the Scriptures and the Symbols. (Respective resolutions of 1932, 1947, 1956; *Lutheran Witness,* Nov. 10, 1953, p. 7 (379); Oct. 7, 1958, p. 15 (471)

Position B
1. Public teachers of the Missouri Synod are sworn to the Sacred Scriptures and the Lutheran Symbols.

2. Therefore public teachers are not bound to further elaborating and safeguarding formulations, such as the Brief Statement.

Respectfully submitted,
Herman Otten
February 8, 1959

―――――――――――

Editor's Note: The name of the professor in the document below has been eliminated since some years later he changed his position.

Redeemer Church
North Tonawanda, N.Y.
March 17, 1958

To whom it may concern:

Whereas the undersigned has long been disturbed by public statements of Dr.__, made in the course of his regular lectures and before many witnesses; and

Whereas the undersigned has not been able to secure an official clarification of the doctrinal issues raised by Dr.__ ; and

Whereas such clarification is now being effected; and

Whereas an effort is being made to limit the scope of this clarification to those issues only which can be documented at first hand by the few persons who are now directly engaged in seeking this clarification; and

Whereas such limitation would ignore and suppress important issues, raised by Dr.__ in his public lectures; and

Whereas the undersigned cannot, at this time, be personally present at the discussions intended to produce the desired clarification;

Therefore I, the undersigned, herewith submit and certify the items which follow, and authorize and request Mr. George F. Lobien to act also in my behalf in securing a complete resolution of these doctrinal concerns, and to take such steps, and to make such use of this document, as may be necessary to achieve the end stated. I am prepared myself to testify to the truth of the statements which follow, and also to name other corroborating witnesses.

The Particulars

In the course of his regular lectures on the Psalms, during the academic year 1956-1957, Dr.__ repeatedly and publicly, in the presence of the class which is now vicaring, and in the presence of the undersigned, defended the position THAT THE NEW TESTAMENT'S HERMENEUTICS AND ISAGOGICS OF THE OLD TESTAMENT IS NOT DOGMATICALLY OBLIGATORY FOR "US." Rather, the NT fills certain OT texts with new meaning. While as Christians we must operate with this new meaning "theologically" and "homiletically," yet as OT interpreters "we" cannot regard this new meaning as the original or historical sense of the OT passage in question. We must not emulate the wooden, inflexible literalism of Fundamentalism. Luther erred in failing to distinguish the OT's original, historical sense and the NT's interpretation thereof.

Specifically

The Psalms which the NT attributes to David were not necessarily written by David. Thereupon the undersigned asked: "Granted that there are some passages in which 'David' could possibly refer merely to a book, i.e. the Psalms, rather than to the person of David, must we not on the basis of St. Matt. 22:41-45 insist, a priori, that at least Psalm 110 was definitely written by David?" Dr.__ replied that the question of Davidic authorship could not be settled a priori from NT passages, but should be answered only on the basis of a strictly scientific study of the internal and external evidence. During the debate that followed, Dr.__ advanced the following arguments in support of his position.

1. In this text Christ was not interested in debating points of isagogics with His opponents. Hence to appeal to this passage as proving the Davidic authorship is to ask it a question which it does not answer.

2. Christ accommodated Himself to the "prevailing views", according to which the Psalter was largely David's work. To the question whether it would not follow from this accommodationism that possibly Christ's whole acceptance of the OT as the authoritative Word of God, as well as His other teachings, were to an unknown extent an "accommodation" to popular notions, no satisfactory reply was given. Dr.__ merely asserted that "abusus non tollit usum," without being able to show how the "usus" of accommodationism could, in principle, be distingushed from the "abusus."

3. "We must take seriously the 'Knechtsgestalt' of Scripture, and Our Lord's state of humiliation. Our Lord and His Apostles were greatly influenced by the prevailing rabbinical hermeneutics." It is true that during subsequent discussions, when pressed with respect to the implications of this argument, in its specific context, for Christology and the teaching

8

authority of Our Lord, Dr.__ neither elaborated on it, nor emphasized it, apparently preferring to base his case on the other arguments. Yet point (3) was never retracted or contradicted by Dr.__.

4. We must not superimpose our Aristoteliam categories upon the primitive, pre-logical (sic) thought-forms of the Bible.

Note: Similarly Dr.__ publicly maintained that Acts 2: 4, 25-31 does not make it dogmatically necessary to maintain the Davidic authorship of Psalm 16; and this despite the facts that

1. St. Peter spoke under direct inspiration of the Holy Ghost, v. 4.

2. St. Peter argues from the Davidic authorship, v. 29.

3. St. Peter asserts not that he is reading a "new," "theological homilet-ical" sense, unknown to David, into the latter's statements (St. Peter's Jewish audience would hardly have been impressed with such sophistry), but that David himself actually "foresaw and spoke of the resurrection of the Christ," v. 31.

B. The same principles apply to the problems in Isaiah, Daniel, Job, Jonah, the Mosaic authorship, etc. These cannot, in principle, be settled a priori by the authority of the NT, but, since they belong to the Bible's "history-side" rather than "faith-side," must be evaluated on the basis of scientifically valid evidence alone.

C. The Old Testament, taken in its literal, original, historical sense, without reading into it later New Testament doctrines, does not teach personal immortality or bodily resurrection, but rather portrays life be-yond the grave as an unhappy, undesirable, shadowlike existence, char-acterized by weakness, darkness, and general unpleasantness. Moreover, this shade-like existence in "Sheol" is shared by the good and evil alike, no distinction being made in this respect. The customary OT proof-texts for resurrection and immortality were dismissed by Dr.__ as inapplicable and irrelevant.

In the fervent hope for a God-pleasing settlement,
Kurt E . Marquart

(Editor's Comment below)

The Theology of Concordia Seminary, St. Louis

Lutheran News, January 15, 1965

In spite of the fact that the faculty of Concordia Seminary attempted to discredit the editor's presentation of doctrinal positions, it was not able to present any evidence that even one statement made by the editor about doctrinal teaching at the St. Louis seminary was in error. In his case with the Faculty and Board of Control of Concordia Seminary before the Board of Appeals of The Lutheran Church-Missouri Synod, the editor was able to furnish documentation to support every statement challenged by the seminary.

The Commission on Theology and Church Relations
Lutheran News, January 14, 1963

The June, 1962 Cleveland Convention of the Missouri Synod established a new "Commission on Theology and Church Relations." On August 1, 1962, the editor sent the document, A SPECIFICATION OF DOCTRINAL ISSUES, to this commission together with the request for an opportunity to present supporting documentation.

He wrote in part:

Although some have challenged the procedure I used in exposing the doctrine taught by certain professors, no one has been able to demonstrate that I misrepresented the doctrinal position maintained by these professors. My counselors and I were able to document every statement I made. Much of this testimony and documentation is contained in the transcript of the Herman Otten vs. Concordia Seminary Case, which is now in my possession.

I have been asked by various officials not to release this transcript for publication, but my conscience will no longer permit me to withhold this valuable evidence that false doctrine is being taught at Concordia Seminary....

One of the points included in the resolution, which established your commission, states:

> While admitting the right of free expression and of public appeal as an inherent right of its members, Synod urges and requests its members to refrain from circularizing Synod or areas thereof until this commission shall have been consulted and a reasonable time shall have been accorded to adjust the matter concerned.

Since I would very much like to follow the procedure established by Synod, would your commission be willing to have me present to it documentation that false doctrine is being taught and tolerated at Concordia Seminary, St. Louis? I am more than willing to appear before your commission during the next two months in order to supply you with such documentation.

Naturally I would have no objections if any of the professors of Concordia Seminary are also present during such a meeting.

On August 9, 1962 the editor received a cordial reply from one of the members of the Praesidium and was assured that his request would be considered by the Commission but that it might take more than two months, since the date of the first meeting of the Commission had not yet been set.

The Commission met on October 24 and 25. In November the Chairman of the Commission assured the Synodical Conference that "All communications addressed to the Commission will be given full consideration."

The editor intends to cooperate with the commission, but he will publish the documentation referred to in his letter to the Commission if he is not granted an opportunity to present this documentation and if no action is taken on the basis of this documentation.

(The CTCR showed no interest in receiving the documentation the editor had showing that false doctrine was being promoted and tolerated in the LCMS. *Lutheran News* (later *Christian News*) began December 15, 1962.)

1. What did the St. Louis professors believe about evolution? ____
2. What is the vicarious satisfaction of Jesus Christ? ____
3. To whom was the ransom paid? ____
4. Are hypocrites and unbelievers members of the Body of Christ? ____
5. The Church in the proper sense of the term is ____.
6. Man consists of ____.
7. Does the Bible teach the immortality of the soul? ____
8. Resurrection means ____.
9. Does the Bible contain errors and contradictions? ____
10. What is Urgeschichte?____
11. What does the New Testament teach about the hermeneutics of the O.T. is ____.
12. The Bible directly predicts ____.
13. Must Christians insist that David wrote Psalms 110 and 16? ____
14. The Scriptural term elect refers to ____.
15. Are public teachers in the LCMS bound to the Brief Statement? ____
16. Are the New Testament hermeneutics and isagogics of the Old Testament dogmatically obligatory? ____
17. Does Matthew 22:41-45 teach that David wrote Psalm 110? ____
18. Does Acts 2:4, 25-31 make it dogmatically necessary to affirm the Davidic authorship of Psalm 16? ____
19. Was the St. Louis faculty able to show "A Specification of Doctrinal Issues" contained error? ____
20. Was the LCMS's Commission on Theology and Church Relations interested in considering documentation of false doctrine at the St. Louis seminary? ____

The LCMS's Real 'Wunderkind" and "Shining Star"

By Herman Otten

When this editor roomed with Dr. Kurt Marquart at Concordia Seminary, St. Louis, Missouri during the 1950's, Jaroslav Pelikan and Martin Marty where considered the LCMS's "wunderkinder," "shining stars," and "intellectual geniuses." They were greatly admired not only by the "liberal intellectual" students but also by many faculty members. Both were featured on the cover of the AAL correspondent, and LCMS youth publications.

At the time the LCMS's real Lutheran Church-Missouri Synod "wunderkind" and "shining star" was 22 year old second year student Kurt Marquart. He was above his liberal professors just as Martin Luther and C.F.W. Walther, "the American Luther," were above the professors and theologians of their day.

Marquart was the chief author of a document submitted to the faculty of Concordia Seminary, St. Louis, on April 30, 1956. It was titled: "A RESPECTFUL, FRIENDLY, BUT URGENT APPEAL TO THE FACULTY." Various faculty members did not believe that any student could have written the appeal without at least the help of some great confessional theologian, possibly Wilhelm Oesch in Germany or Paul Burgdorf, editor of the *Confessional Lutheran*. This editor can testify that the entire document is almost exclusively the work of the young Kurt Marquart. Even at that time he "outshown" Dr. Arthur Carl Piepkorn and Dr. Richard Caemmerer who 50 years ago were considered by many the greatest intellects on the seminary campus. Student Marquart showed that Piepkorn's view of ordination and election was contrary to the Bible and that Caemmerer denied the scriptural doctrine of the vicarious satisfaction of Christ.

The document shows that there is not much difference between the young Marquart and the mature Marquart who was called to his eternal home 50 years after he wrote the appeal. It was one of the exhibits the editor of *Christian News* presented to the Board of Control of Concordia Seminary on December 4, 1958 when he appealed the decision of the faculty of Concordia Seminary preventing him from entering the ministry of the LCMS. Kurt Marquart served as the editor's chief counsel in this case. Others were Dr. Siegbert Becker, at that time a professor at Concordia Teachers College, River Forest, and Rev. H. W. Niewald, the pastor of Bethlehem Lutheran Church, New Haven, Missouri.

The editor intended to include this document at Concordia Seminary, St. Louis as an appendix to the banquet speech he prepared to present to the 2006 Walther Conference on November 10, the birthday of Martin

Luther. The old chapel at the Seminary would have been a dramatic place to present Marquart's 50 year old appeal to the faculty on Luther's birthday. The editor's speech, which will be published in a future issue of *Christian News*, shows why CN has called Marquart "The International Luther." The speech will not be presented at the seminary because the LCMS's "International Center" ordered the seminary not to allow the Walther Conference to be held at the seminary. Student Marquart quoted the seminary's student publication, *The Seminarian,* to show what kind of liberal theology was being permitted at the seminary. Some even referred to this publication as the "Semi-Arian."

Marquart was in line to become the editor of the *The Seminarian* but he was cheated out of becoming editor through some unethical tactics by students Robert Wilken and Richard John Neuhaus. The CN editor let students Wilken and Neuhaus, who are now Roman Catholics, know what he thought about their dishonest ethics. Marquart was the only student who applied for the position of editor before the announced deadline for applications. In no way were Wilken and Neuhaus, who along with the CN editor had done some writing for *The Seminarian,* going to allow Marquart to be editor. After the deadline passed for applications they asked one of their liberal cronies, far less qualified than Marquart, to submit an application which was then quickly accepted.

Neither the liberals on the faculty or among the students wanted the LCMS real "wunderkind" and "shining star," the author of the "A RESPECTFUL FRIENDLY, BUT URGENT APPEAL TO THE FACULTY" (below) to be the editor of the seminary's student publication.

Christian News, November 6, 2006

A RESPECTFUL, FRIENDLY, BUT URGENT APPEAL TO THE FACULTY

Reverend Sirs and Fathers in Christ:

Impelled by the Easter issue of our campus journal, the Seminarian, as immediate cause, we beg leave to bring to your attention matters which have greatly disturbed us and others for some time now. In the estimation of the undersigned the theological situation on our campus is definitely critical, and this to a greater extent than can be accounted for by the margin of human weakness to be expected in any orthodox church body. Permit us therefore to summarize, as briefly as possible, the theological issues which, on the basis of, two years' candid observation of conditions at this Seminary, are of the acutest concern to us.

Our concern is not so much with particular doctrines, such as for instance Verbal Inspiration, essential as this doctrine is, but with a much more fundamental matter, namely with a basic approach to theology, which we believe to be at the bottom of whatever other, more particular theological difficulties may be troubling our campus:

PART I

1) THE NATURE OF THE TRUTH

Due to a sustained and apparently unopposed influx of neo-orthodox-Lundensian propaganda there exists a marked tendency to regard "truth," "Word," "Gospel," "doctrine," and the like not as possessing objective, propositional, thetical content, but rather as constituting various indefinable aspects of some vague, essentially subjective, non-rational "experience" or "encounter," which is inevitably described as "existential." We are aware of the fact that this tendency manifests itself in varying degrees and forms, not all of which are necessarily or intrinsically unsalutary. Its usual form, however, in our experience, has been the threefold claim that a) Orthodox (including old-Missourian) theology, being based on "Aristotelian scholastic" philosophy is incongruent with both Biblical and contemporary "thought forms" and hence its formulations possess, to say the least with much charity, a high degree of irrelevance; b) The Biblical concept of "truth" is "alogical" or "pre-logical," in antithesis to the Greek idea of " truth" as something that is correct or factually true; c) language itself is very relative and tentative, and hence no particular formulation ought to be insisted upon.

The far-reaching implications of such a modus loquendi, whose strength and appeal lies in its operation with half-truths, can hardly be

14

overestimated. If applied with any appreciable degree of consistency, this "approach," by a necessity inherent in its very nature, renders meaningless any and all Confessional statements. It is its sweeping, radical nature that makes this approach so dangerous. For it means that, what is challenged is not a particular doctrine, but the entire theological structure of Confessional Lutheranism. This makes the detection of resultant doctrinal errors extremely difficult, at least if one is determined to regard only the explicit rejection of a specific doctrine as proof of doctrinal aberration; for such a rejection may never become explicit, and yet the entire orthodox theology be all along regarded as irrelevant!

A logical and actual concomitant of the tendency here outlined is the constant demand for "restatement" of theological truth in the "thought forms" of today. Now nothing could make us happier than just such a restatement, carried through conscientiously, thoroughly, and consistently; for it would mean clear, explicit formulation and definition of the orthodox position in antithesis to all modern errors, including those of the neo-orthodox-Lundensian Schwaermer. But our experience has shown, and we do not care to generalize beyond our own experience, that this is far from what the proponents of "restatement in the thought forms of today" usually contemplate. They often do not venture beyond a general affirmation of the irrelevance of past dogmatic terminology. The writings of orthodox theologians of the past, and especially the works of Dr. Pieper, including even the Brief Statement (!) tend to be viewed in a "detached," "objective" manner which suggests the attitude of an antiquarian scrutinizing a particularly curious specimen of days long gone by. It is said: "We are not bound to the views or terminology of Pieper." Very correct, properly understood. But the careless, frequent, and general appeal to this principle causes us to ask cautiously: To which views, and to which terminology of Pieper are we not bound? Obviously, if Pieper was an orthodox theologian, one cannot disagree with all or most of his "views" and still remain orthodox. As for the matter of terminology, is there not, due to the very nature of language, a point at which the connection between form and content becomes so close that a rejection of the former involves denial of the latter?

Was it not against the "unruhigen, zankgierigen Leute, so an keine gewisse Form der reinen Lehr gebunden sein wollen" that the Lutheran Confessors found it necessary to adopt clear thetical and antithetical Symbols, from which they pledged themselves "gar nicht, weder in rebus, noch in phrasibus, abzuweichen, sondern vielmehr durch die Gnade des Heiligen Geistes einmutiglich dabei zu verharren und zu bleiben, auch alle Religionsstreit und deren Erklarungen danach zu regulieren. . . ?" (Preface to the F. C.)

Specific attempts at the reformulation in the "thought forms of today" have in our experience taken the following forms, which we here list as examples:

a) The Real Presence: It is "Aristotelian" to speak of the presence of our Lord's actual body and blood under the species of bread and wine in the Holy Eucharist. All we can say is that in the Sacrament Christ comes

15

to us.

b) The Trinity: Some anti-"Aristotelian" discussions of the Holy Trinity give the impression, in the words of one disturbed observer, "as if the doctrine of the Trinity was gotten up in private between Pieper and Aristotle."

c) The Vicarious Satisfaction (!): Denial of the vicarious satisfaction does not involve denial of the atonement. The latter is conceivable without the former. We must not present God as an angry tyrant demanding satisfaction of His justice. God's justice, in distinction to His love, is but a figure of speech, as also are the terms "ransom" and "sacrifice." We do not know to whom the ransom was paid. The atonement means that God in love reestablished fellowship with men.

2) THE CERTAINTY OF TRUTH

Due to such views, which regard truth as some aspect of a basically subjective religious experience, and not as objective subject-matter to be didactically transmitted and zealously guarded, the certainty of truth, that which our synodical forefathers were accustomed to call Lehrgewissheit, has to an alarming extent disappeared from among us.

To be certain of the correctness of one's doctrinal position and to act in accordance with this conviction is regarded as insufferable conceit and arrogance, if not as naive, unenlightened provincialism. On the other hand applause and commendation are the reward of "objectivity," "open-mindedness," and "maturity," virtues which under the circumstances we cannot but characterize as theological agnosticism, because their proponents appear to reduce what the Lutheran Church has always taught as doctrines to "questions," "exegetical problems," etc. The doctrine of inspiration becomes the problem of inspiration, the doctrine of Church and Ministry becomes the question of Church and Ministry, etc. By some curious process of rationalization the lack of Lehrgewissheit is lauded as a mark of humility, maturity and love. After all, how can we "presume" to know God's truth? Are we not also in theology simul justi et peccatores?

We believe that this sort of approach breathes an altogether "different spirit"—different to the point of incompatibility—from the one that animated the old Missouri Synod. What C. F. W. Walther said in utter disgust, about extra-synodical conditions, especially in speculative Germany, is NOW ALSO TRUE OF OUR OWN SEMINARY: "This thesis divides into two parts. The one part demands that a pure teacher present all the articles of the Faith in accordance with Scripture (schriftgemaess). Now this is an unheard of demand in our day. People, even so-called believers, are horrified, when someone says: 'I have found the truth, I am certain in every doctrine of revelation.' Such a claim is regarded as an arrogance. Especially a young student must not say that of himself. 'Only don't be finished!' They call to you in Germany, 'Don't believe that you have already found the truth! Just keep on studying, until you have reached the goal!' . . .for they fear that one might be finished with any one article, rather than continuing forever to roll the stone, to lift it up. Therefore also Kahnis, who had formerly been truly Lutheran, tried to

16

justify himself in the preface to his miserable dogmatics, in the words: 'Dies diem docet,' with which he wants to say: 'A year ago I believed this and that, but then other thoughts came to me, then I found other doctrines.' A miserable, horrible position? No, God's Word demands that we should have it completely pure and clear, so that we can say, when we leave the pulpit: 'I have preached God's Word aright, that I can swear to it, yea, that if an angel came from heaven. I could still say: I have preached aright!' Therefore Luther says, though in paradoxical manner, that when a preacher leaves the pulpit he may not pray an Our Father, but he should do that before the sermon; for a true preacher does not need to say after the sermon: 'Forgive me my debt,' but: 'I have proclaimed the pure truth.' But nowadays, when one says that, one is regarded as half-mad. So deeply people are sunk in skepticism. . .

"When it is said: 'One never gets to the point that one can present the article of the Faith scripturally (schriftgemaess),' then this is a devilish doctrine. Especially when the students hear it, is it a veritable hellish poison which is given into their hearts; then they will be not at all diligent to get to the bottom of the truth, to become clear about the truth." (Gesetz und Evangelium, pp. 28-29)

Yet this "Hollengift," this "teuflische Lehre" enjoys popularity on this campus as the only sensible, realistic, and in fact inescapable position. In contrast to our synodical fathers, who viewed Sacred Theology as a habitus practicus, something which was essentially simple, corresponding to the child-like nature of Christian faith, something which laymen had a right and duty to Judge, our modern theological thought is too humble to claim to know the truth. Theology is rather regarded as infinitely complex, as essentially speculative, as something which is so esoteric that no layman can ever hope to discriminate between true and false doctrine. In fact, even theologians, it seems, cannot and must not provide much more effective criteria of orthodoxy than the frequency with which the name "Christ" occurs in a given theological treatise!

One of the most insidious attacks on Lehrgewissheit is the "humble" claim that while Scripture itself may be the objective and infallible revelation of God, yet we can never be sure that we understand Scripture correctly, for the closest we can get to Scripture is in our own interpretation. Naturally, as soon as it is conceded that the doctrine of the Evangelical Lutheran Church rests not on the perspicuous Scripture itself, but on some particular, not necessarily correct interpretation thereof, then Lehrgewissheit indeed becomes papistic arrogance and hence impossible of attainment.

And so it is that we find Pilate's question, "What is truth?" and the devil's suggestion of the "epistemological problem," "Yea, hath God said?" reiterated in all seriousness on this campus. The question, what is orthodoxy?, is regarded as rhetorical, i.e. as one which only a presumptuous obscurantist will attempt to answer dogmatically.

PART II: PRACTICAL CONCLUSIONS

We believe that the present theological confusion on our campus cannot be eliminated effectively except by decided and deliberate action of the faculty, to whom the students do and must look for competent guidance, under God and His Scripture, toward all truth and away from all error. We intensely wish to avoid the appearance as though we would presume to prescribe to the faculty how to fulfill their duties. But because we feel that as students we are closer to the "grass-roots" and more directly in touch with the problem situation under discussion, and also because personal contact with individual faculty members convinces us that they conceive of the problem as consisting merely in a few students doubting a few specific doctrines, or going through the usual processes of intellectual maturation, therefore we feel a compelling need to localize and focus as sharply as possible the particular theological sore-spots that require treatment. We are convinced that if more than a few superficial symptoms are to be treated, the faculty must not only possess, but also vigorously publicize, in lectures, in all classes, private counsel, and written presentations — to the point of tiresome reiteration, if need be — a clear, unequivocal, uncompromising, and above all unanimous stand with regard to at least the following issues:

1) **THE NATURE OF TRUTH:** We are deeply aware of the salutary Scriptural, Lutheran principle that in purely philosophical questions the Church has no right to speak. But in this matter the basic question is eminently theological and can be stated, at the risk of oversimplification, as follows: IS TRUTH STATEMENTS OR IS IT SOMETHING ELSE, i.e A PERSON, EXPERIENCE, etc.? We believe that an honest answer to this question belongs not simply to the bene esse or the plene esse, but to the very ESSE of orthodox theology. For on the answer to this question depends whether the distinction between true and false doctrine is valid, or whether truth and error are merely matters of "emphasis," "trend," "tendency," "insight," "motif," etc.

In connection with this matter, does the Missouri Synod still believe, teach and confess doctrines, or does it leave the matter largely to the discretion of each pastor's "insight?" Are orthodox teachers still bound to the Symbolical Books in rebus et phrasibus? Are orthodox teachers and confessional documents still expected to set forth the pure Word of God itself, though in extra-Biblical terms, or are they expected merely to approach the Word of God? Are orthodox theological formulations to be regarded as correct restatements of divine truth itself, or are they merely historically-conditioned approximation, "in, with, and under" which the real truth is to be sought?

As regards publica doctrina, does the Missouri Synod still teach, permit, and tolerate only one publica doctrina? Above all, does the BRIEF STATEMENT still represent the official position of the Missouri Synod, to the exclusion of all antitheses? Is it proper and permissible to regard the Brief Statement as abrogated (i. e. as official position) in all those points which are not explicitly reiterated in the Common Confession? Is the Brief Statement's doctrine binding in conscience upon every public teacher of Synod, also with regard to Holy Scripture, the Trinity, Election and Conversion, Creation, Church, Ministry, and Ordination, Open Questions, or is it possible for a non-unionistic Synod to have an official position which is binding upon no one in particular, but only on "Synod in general?" Is it proper and permissible to regard only those points of doctrine as binding which are explicitly taught in the Lutheran Symbols, or is the acceptance of all Scriptural doctrines, including all those listed in the Brief Statement, still required for church fellowship in and with the Missouri Synod?

2) THE CERTAINTY OF TRUTH: Can and must a Scriptural theologian be certain of the truth of his theological position, to the exclusion of all antitheses? Does the Missouri Synod still acknowledge with Dr. Pieper the following position as the only possible one, or will it now permit this position to be derided and denounced as presumption and obscurantism:

"The Christian Church is no philosophers' school. In the philosophers' school the pro and con are considered, and then it is usually agreed to let the matter rest undecided—and that is the most sensible. . . . The Christian Church, as such, does not deal with anything but certainty. Insofar as an ecclesiastical fellowship teaches uncertainties, presents doubtful matters, or stimulates doubt, it does not have the divinely intended character of the Christian Church. The Christian Church does not just seek the truth, but it has the truth. It makes a great impression upon inexperienced people when someone says: 'The Christians should not claim with such certainty that they have the truth, but should admit that they are sincerely endeavoring to find the truth. It therefore does not behoove Christians so definitely to deny the right of existence to deviating views, etc.' What folly! The Christian Church is not a society for the discovery of the saving truth, but a society for the proclamation of the saving truth. . . In an essay I had expressed among other things, the sentence; 'We cannot err, or are INFALLIBLE in doctrine, INASMUCH AS AND BECAUSE WE STAND ON GOD'S WORD AS IT READS.' This sentence has been making the rounds in Germany for two years. People pretend to be horrified over it. One should hardly consider it possible that the correctness of this sentence is doubted within Christendom. Is there then, any truth at all yet in the world, if one can err even WHEN ONE STANDS ON GOD'S WORD AS IT READS? WHEN ONE SPEAKS GOD'S WORD AS IT READS? Then everything ceases, then we close the Bible and many other books, also our churches we close then, and say with Pilate, 'What is truth?'

"Incidentally, I had quite explicitly guarded myself against all misunderstanding. I want to read to you what I said then. In the report of the year 1888 it says on page 18 'We admit, that we personally can err, yes, that we, if it depended on us, can only err in spiritual matters. But IN DOCTRINE we do not err but are infallible, INASMUCH AS AND BE-

CAUSE WE STAND ON GOD'S WORD AS IT READS. . . . THE
LUTHERAN CHURCH CLAIMS TO BE IN THE POSSESSION OF THE
CERTAIN, ENTIRE TRUTH ONLY BECAUSE SHE ACCEPTS THE
CERTAIN, ENTIRE WORD OF GOD, AS IT READS.' . . . Don't let yourself be pushed out of this Lutheran position; otherwise you must cast
yourselves into the sea of uncertainty. It is said: Yes, but God's Word may
be variously interpreted. That is not true. God's Word cannot be variously
interpreted, but God's Word in a definite context has always only ONE
definite sense: and we stand not on the INTERPRETATIONS of the Word
of God, given by men, but on GOD'S WORD ITSELF. . . When we Lutherans arrange colloquia with other church-bodies, we can never do that in
the sense as if through these colloquia it should first become certain for
us, what is truth and what is error. We know that beforehand." (Vortraege, pp. 143-165)

3) NEO*ORTHODOXY, EXISTENTIALISM, LUNDENSIANISM:
Through their written works such men as Barth, Brunner, Tillich, Aulen,
Nygren, and others, are teaching almost as effectively on this campus as
if they had been formally called to this seminary as theological professors.
We believe that the influence of these individuals will never be broken
unless and until the faculty takes a public and unanimous stand regarding their errors, and makes systematic efforts to implement this stand.

We are quite desperate in our request for such a stand, because it appears to us that no serious, definite, decisive attempt at meeting the challenge of the new theology is being made in behalf of orthodox
Lutheranism. The only such attempt which we know of is the valiant,
single-handed effort of Dr. Hamann of our Australian sister synod. While
we are aware of the fact that the average seminarian on our campus has
a healthy suspicion for esoteric and speculative theologies, we believe
that all of our future pastors need to be enabled to detect the differences
between orthodox theology and contemporary systems, and to defend, the
former effectively. This defense cannot, we believe, be carried on, except
by a restatement of orthodox theology in the terms provided by the antitheses, and a consistent application of the principles of orthodox
Lutheranism to modern aberrations. General, well-meaning exhortations
to "heed the Word" or "obey Christ" are quite useless, we believe, because
the neologists delight in the use of euphemistic platitudes and are perfectly willing to accommodate themselves to orthodox terminology. What
is needed is an incisive expose of the radical differences in intent behind
the use of largely identical expressions by the orthodox and the neologists
respectively. Likewise needed is a categorical affirmation and application
of the principles that a) anyone who rejects the Vicarious Satisfaction
thereby places himself extra ecclesiam (Pieper, *Christliche Dogmatik*, I,
p. 90) and b) "We hold that all teachers and communions that deny the
doctrine of the Holy Trinity are outside the pale of the Christian Church"
(Brief Statement, #4).

As for "existentialism," we are again not asking for a definition of an
"official philosophy" in antithesis to existentialism (which latter seems

20

to be beyond definition anyway) but we are asking for clear, understandable guide-lines which would indicate and specify those forms or concomitants (actual or conceivable) of existentialism which are definitely not and can never be acceptable to orthodox theology.

4) THE SEMINARIAN: Regarding our campus journal, *The Seminarian*, we beg leave to submit the following:

The magazine appears to us to be a consistent advocate of a theology of uncertainty. The publication seems to us to be symptomatic of the trend we have been outlining above. Witness the radical difference between the quotations from Walther and Pieper adduced by us and sentiments such as the following, from this year's issues of the Seminarian:

a) "The simple and painless way of dismissing this spectacle is to claim that one has the only true interpretation of the scripture himself, while all other interpretations represent aberrations. Indeed, one could even claim that all other viewpoints and groups were based upon interpretations of the Scriptures, whereas his viewpoint and group were based upon the Scriptures themselves, without any interpretation necessary." (Reformation Day, p. 35)

b) "....those profound evangelical insights in the Confessions by which much of systematic theology has been fundamentally questionable." (ibid., p. 36)

c) "....you'll never again be able to feel that the last word has been said on anything, nor that you know all there is to know about any problem, not even that you are familiar with all the literature on the problem. That's bound to make your existence as a theologian somewhat insecure; whether it also makes it richer is up to you." (Epiphany, p. 10)

d) "More than this, he may be using these doubts to make your patient less indoctrinated and opinionated in his faith. You must guard against this at all costs. If your patient stops thinking he possesses all truth in a nutshell, he is likely to become charitable and sympathetic with those that disagree with him. When this sort of thing runs rampant, the Church might become a positive hot-bed of love and mutual understanding." (Epiphany, p. 22)

e) "This study makes us wonder if it is worth striving after the elusive goal of objectivity. Perhaps theology is going down a blind alley when it seeks certainty in the realm of knowing. Some theologians seek the answer in some form of compromise between objectivity and subjectivity, and others want to lift the problem up into the realm of being and becoming rather than knowing. Both methods deserve our consideration" (Epiphany, p. 31) NOTE: Pending the outcome of personal dealings with the author of the article in question, we refrain from listing other grave objections to statements in this article.

f) "Remaining apart, with the conviction that the Missouri Synod has possession of the fullness of truth — this was one (!) view of our relationship toward the WCC. This particular (!) view was pointedly expressed in a LUTHERAN WITNESS editorial of August 31, 1954. Since this is the only article of its kind (!), and appears in our synodical house-organ, it is quoted here in full: 'If the Missouri Synod is included in the second charge, we plead guilty. We are in conscience convinced that we have the full truth. We believe in no development of doctrines. We believe that the fullness of truth has been revealed in God's complete revelation. Holy Scripture.'" (Easter, p. 32)

We realize that some of these quotes would, taken by themselves, be capable of perfectly acceptable interpretation — provided they were offset by equally explicit affirmation of the objectivity and certainty of orthodox theology, along the lines of our quotes from Walther and Pieper. But in the absence of such neutralizing statements we cannot but regard these quotes as symptomatic of the modern theological agnosticism which is essentially the same as the skepticism which already Walther had to face, HOWEVER, AT THAT TIME OUTSIDE OUR OWN SYNOD!

We fail to see any real difference between the theology of the Seminarian issues of the last two years and the controversial article "Orthodoxy Against Itself" in the June, 1954 issue, which caused such offense in our Synod. The difference appears to us to be merely a matter of degree, not of kind. What "Orthodoxy Against Itself" said with relative clarity, consistency, and honesty - and we cannot consider that article as retracted or corrected by the "Note" in the August, 1955 issue, because we believe that the article did much more than merely "lead to misunderstanding overstate his case. . . .misjudge conditions in our Synod, etc." — other articles have been implying ever since. In fact even if all objectionable quotes adduced by us were to be eliminated, we would still object that there is not much, if anything at all, in the last two years' issues of the Seminarian which is definitely incompatible with a watery sort of U.L.C. "Lutheranism." We noted a deplorable lack of doctrinal conviction, an approving attitude toward heretical theologians (cf. April, 1955, pp. 16 and 18; August, 1955, pp. 20, 21: May, 1955, pp. 25-26; January, 1956, p. 23), an atavistic preoccupation with exhortations and "social issues" which seem to attend the waning of doctrinal convictions and a sustained, one-sided propaganda in favor of the ecumenical movement.

As regards the latter item, we wish to take this opportunity to protest against the publication of biased, pro-ecumenical material in the last (Easter, 1956) issue, which became the proximate cause for this letter. We are convinced, and are confident that we can prove our contention, that the World Council of Churches proclaims Christians and public infidels and heathens brothers "in Christ." We therefore believe that at least in this case II Cor. 6, 14-17 applies with full force. For this reason we believe that we have no more right to join the World Council of Churches than to become Freemasons, the witnessing argument being equally irrelevant in both cases, and we earnestly and decidedly reject and repudiate pro-W.C.C. propaganda and protest strenuously against the publication of such propaganda in our Seminarian. We consider this a giving, not a taking of offense.

The dangerous spirit of the Seminarian was, we believe, conclusively revealed by last year's experiment with "Another Voice." We definitely recall that at the time when "Another Voice" was begun, the then editor of the Seminarian told us personally that the purpose of "Another Voice" was to give those an opportunity to express themselves, whose views were admittedly DIFFERENT from those of the Seminarian staff. What was actually printed in the Seminarian's "Another Voice?" Very wholesome articles, setting forth the orthodox position with regard to Verbal Inspiration, the Lutheran Symbols, etc. Notable is the fact that such articles were not printed in the rest of the Seminarian, but were consigned to "Another Voice" as if they represented merely a permissible divergent opinion!

That this was not merely our subjective impression, became definitely established for as when we were shown a letter from a prominent graduate of the previous year, who had been "in the know of things". In this letter he praises the Seminarian highly, but then asks what "Another Voice" is doing in the Seminarian, and whether this is an attempt to placate the "reactionaries" (sic)!

We believe we can confidently challenge anyone to demonstrate that the articles which appeared in "Another Voice" were more "reactionary" than the position which the Missouri Synod has always taken. If those views are reactionary, then what is the "normal" position?

To quote a few uncorrected statements from last year's Seminarian:

a.) "One cannot square the emphasis of the Gospel proclamation with the emphasis of modern orthodoxy." (Christmas, 1955, p. 35)

b) ". . .so also theology bears only an incidental relation to the object of its investigation, the faith of the Christian Church. It may contain certain immutables, but it cannot be 'true' or 'untrue'", (ibid.,. p. 40)

c) "Doctrinal unity between the Missouri Synod and the American Lutheran Church has already been established, and their differences resolved on the principle that there are certain non -fundamental doctrines of Holy Scripture (!) which need not be divisive of church fellowship." (August, 1955, p. 19) NOTE: If this statement is true, then why the strenuous opposition to the charges of the Wisconsin and Norwegian Synods? If it is false, why has it not been challenged?

To repeat, we see merely a difference of degree between this year's and last year's Seminarian. Since the thing to which we object is more a fundamental approach, a basic view of theology, than a denial of a set of particular doctrines, we believe that for purposes of censorship it is inadequate to regard only an explicit rejection of a specific doctrine as proof of theological unsoundness.

We believe that it is legitimate and even necessary to object not only to explicit statements, but also to implications. We believe that it is appropriate to find implications in theological articles, not indeed arbitrarily, but on the basis of considerations such as the following: 1) Contemporary theological developments and terminology in the area under discussion. 2) Such known views of the writer as might throw light on the article. 3) Significant omissions, i.e. failure to rule out obvious possibilities suggested by the article. 4) General tone and emphasis. For instance we would be suspicious of a presentation which consistently praises Arius and criticizes Athanasius in the area of the doctrine of

Christ, even though the presentation did not explicitly reject orthodox Christology. 5) Possible intent behind a statement that is so obvious as to justify the assumption that some other, more controversial matter is really meant.

On the basis of all the preceding we respectfully request that until such time as the editors of the Seminarian may see fit to produce something more than a magazine that, due to its advocacy of theological uncertainty could appropriately be published at any U.L.C. seminary, the publication of said Seminarian be suspended.

PART III: QUALIFICATIONS

1) We are not requesting a reply to this appeal to us personally. Our sole purpose is to call to the faculty's attention the particular issues which in our estimation and on the basis of our observation require clarification if the theological chaos on our campus is to be resolved.

2) We are not herewith accusing any individuals. We are indicting ways of thinking which we consider to be mortal foes of orthodox theology.

3) We are not of the number of those whose main interest is the scrupulous observance of the letter of Synodical regulations of practice. We believe that in the past, members of Synod have been guilty of indefensible legalism in some areas of practice. We do not wish a repetition of such instances.

4) We do not wish to disparage Christian charity in the least, and indeed it would be blasphemy to do so. We wholeheartedly believe that Christian love is to be applied under any circumstances, theological controversies not excluded.

5) We have not written this letter under the delusion that we ourselves are in any way perfect or "better" than anyone else.

6) Rather it is BECAUSE we realize our utter sinfulness and unworthiness, that we cling so desperately to that which alone is firm, immovable, objective, reliable, and unchanging in a world of flux and illusion, namely the pure Scriptural faith of the Evangelical Lutheran Church, which at Holy Confirmation we have sworn to uphold. It is BECAUSE we realize our limitations, and BECAUSE we know that we are men and not God, that we believe with our synodical forefathers that only "Repristinations theologie" has a right to exist, that pastors and teachers must present God's truth purely and entirely, that they must be absolutely certain of their theological position, for Christian consciences demand certainty, that ONLY God's truth has a right to be taught in the Church, and that therefore ANY and EVERY persistent doctrinal error, whether fundamental or non-fundamental, is divisive of church fellowship.

7) We do not wish to minimize the danger of theological Pharisaism, but we can no more regard this danger as an excuse for the absence of Lehrgewissheit, than we can consider the constant temptation to self-

righteousness inherent in sanctification an excuse for riotous living.

8) We realize that, humanly speaking, it looks absolutely terrible for two second-year theological upstarts to undertake what we have here undertaken. Therefore, we have not acted rashly in this matter, but only in accordance with the irresistible demands of conscience, as it were unwillingly. We, therefore, beg your indulgence and wish all attention to be directed away from our persons and to the issues themselves. For this reason we would have preferred — if it were not dishonorable — to submit this appeal anonymously.

9) We are quite sure of this, that we are not hereby raising original problems or new issues. The conflict is not between present conditions and ourselves, but between present conditions and our synodical past. The initiative in raising this issue is to be imputed not to us, but to the innovations.

10) Finally, our appeal to you, our fathers in the faith, is not based ultimately on such trifles as our legal membership in the Lutheran Church-Missouri Synod or our formal enrollment at this seminary, but on the fact that by God's grace we are and intend to remain Christians. Although, we could have secured many signatures for this letter – for there is an increasing number of students who are worried about the present theological confusion—we refrained from doing so, lest we give the appearance of attempting to precipitate "mob-action." In fact we do not even submit this letter on the basis of our own signatures, as if they mattered, but alone on the basis of the objective, intrinsic importance of the matters involved. These we humbly beg to be considered, in the name of Our Lord Jesus Christ, the Supreme Doctor of Sacred Theology.

Concordia Seminary
St. Louis, Missouri

SOME IMPORTANT DOCTRINE

I. The Holy Scriptures

1. Whether the Holy Scriptures are, in all their parts and words, the very Word of God, communicated to the sacred writers by the Holy Ghost.

2. Whether these Holy Scriptures are entirely true and without error in all matters of which they treat, including geographical, historical, and other secular matters.

3. Whether all the events described in the first few chapters of the Book of Genesis, including the Creation, Adam and Eve, the Fall into Sin, etc. are historically and literally factual and correct, as described.

4. Whether there is any objection to the Brief Statement's formulation of Verbal Inspiration (Paragraphs 1-3).

II. Ministry and Ordination

1. Whether the spiritual priests of a Christian congregation are the original and immediate possessors of all Church power (i.e. administra-

tion of all the means of grace), or whether this power, or any part thereof, is originally and immediately vested in the ministerium.

2. Whether the office of the ministry is validly conferred by the call of a Christian Congregation, even without the imposition of hands by an ordained clergyman in Holy Ordination.

3. Whether God confers the ministerial office through the congregation's delegation of its priestly powers, or through the imposition of hands by a clergyman.

4. Whether, other things being equal, the Ordination imparted by a clergyman who is himself un-ordained or improperly ordained, is valid.

5. Whether the Holy Sacraments are always valid, and efficacious whenever administered under the auspices of the orthodox Confession, irrespective of the administrant's ordination or lack of it.

III. The Holy Trinity

1. Whether the term "Person" in the confessional formula "Three Persons in one Godhead" is to be taken as meaning a distinct "I" (Ego) or self-consciousness.

2. Whether the corresponding antithesis is to be regarded as a denial of the doctrine.

IV. The Real Presence

1. Whether the heavenly elements of the true body and the true blood of our Lord Jesus Christ are actually and substantially present, by virtue of sacramental union, with the earthly Eucharistic elements of the bread and wine respectively.

2. Whether this presence of the heavenly elements of our Lord's body and blood is unique to the Sacrament of the Altar, i.e. not merely of the nature of Christ's presence with the Word, or in the hearts of His believers, or in the universe in general.

3. Whether the true body and blood of Christ are received in the Sacrament with the mouth of the body, so that this oral reception is essentially distinct from the reception of Christ by faith in the heart.

4. Whether the true body and blood of Christ are orally received in the Sacrament by all communicants, also by the impenitent and the unworthy, namely to their judgment.

(Ed. Note: This article is included in "Concordia Seminary, St. Louis vs. Otten Case – Book of Documentation, Arranged by Kurt Marquart", *Christian News, November 6, 2006*)

1. Who were the Lutheran Church-Missouri Synod's "wunderkinder" and "shining stars" in the 1950s? _____
2. Who were considered by many to be the greatest intellects on the faculty of Concordia Seminary? _____
3. How much difference is there between the views of the "young" Marquart and the "mature" Marquart? _____
4. Who ordered Concordia Seminary, St. Louis, not to allow the Walther

26

Conference to be held at the seminary? _____
5. Some referred to the Seminarian as the _____.
6. Who cheated Marquart out of becoming editor of the Seminarian?
_____
7. The theological situation at Concordia Seminary is _____.
8. What was at the bottom of the theological difficulties at the
    seminary?_____
9. What was being challenged was not a particular doctrine but _____.
10. How was the vicarious satisfaction of Christ being denied? _____
11. The _____ of truth was disappearing.
12. What C.F.W. Walther said about conditions in speculative Germany
    is now also true about _____.
13. What was being reiterated on the campus of the St. Louis seminary
    about truth? _____
14. Does the _____ still represent the official position of the LCMS?
15. The Christian Church is not _____ school.
16. The Christian Church does not _____ the truth but _____ the truth.
17. Through their written works who were teaching effectively at
    Concordia Seminary? _____
18. All future pastors should be enabled to _____.
19. What was Dr. Hamann of Australia doing? _____
20. The Seminarian was an advocate of _____
21. The World Council of Churches proclaims _____.
22. In the past some members of the LCMS have been guilty of _____.
23. Only _____ has the right to exist.
24. Is the Bible without error in all matters? _____
25. Does God confer the ministerial office through the call of a congre-
    gation or through ordination? _____
26. Is the term "Person" in the Holy Trinity to be taken to mean distinct
    "I"? _____
27. Are the true body and blood received by all communicants? _____

RESPONSE TO LCMS PLEA
TO SUPPORT VALPARAISO

Dr. John W. Behnken, President
The Lutheran Church-Missouri Synod
Dear Dr. Behnken:
The other day I received your appeal in behalf of Valparaiso University. I wanted to send just a brief response, but the more I thought about it, the longer the response became for Valparaiso is but an aspect of a much larger situation. Believe me, I do not intend to weary you with long letters as a matter of habit. This shall be the first and last, barring unforeseen circumstances. And I do not wish to pontificate to my President. I know that from your vantage-point things may look different, and that you do not owe me an accounting for your views or actions. Still I cannot avoid the duty to speak, freely and honestly, when I believe the welfare of the Church to be at stake. Please, therefore, accept these jottings as expressions of burning concerns — of long standing, I might add — expressed by a young under-shepherd to his ecclesiastical superior in love, respect, and confidence.

Well, first about Valparaiso. I think I can imagine a weary knowing look steal across your face as I tell you that I could not possibly support Valparaiso either morally or financially. I'm sure I needn't tell you why. And I do believe in the ideal of a great Lutheran University. But Valparaiso is no longer that. I'd rather see Christ's lambs entrusted to my care, exposed to the honestly anti-Christian or at least non-Christian influences of secular schools than to the rank modernism and skepticism arrogantly championed by Valparaiso's *Cresset* under the sacrilegious disguise of the Lutheran name. And I happen to know a little more about Valparaiso than what appears in the *Cresset,* and that knowledge is not conductive to a peaceful conscience!

Of course I know that you can't be blind to the situation there. If you do lend that institution the unquestioned prestige of your name, you do it in the firm hope that all is not lost yet, and that "Valpo" can still be saved. Of course you know much better than I do, exactly what ways are open to Synod to secure the University's compliance with the Lutheran Confession, not to say the Christian religion. Yet, barring a miracle, upon which we have no right to presume, it seems to me, from my little corner, that Valparaiso is lost, lost irrevocably, to the Lutheran Church. The cancer must be cut quickly, before it poisons the whole organism. In fact, we will be lucky— to use a trite, secular phrase—if St. Louis can still be saved for the Church!

It seems to me that the one hope for Valparaiso would be prompt, radical action, preferably by Synodical officials. Private efforts will be smeared as witch-hunts, etc. However, if something rather decisive is not done soon, it would become necessary for private interested persons to prepare and publish a complete brief, with *Cresset* quotations and other written evidence, on the basis of which Synod would be memorialized to confront the University with the ultimatum: Either the doctrinal mess is resolved immediately, by means of mass resignations, if necessary (of the strength of character demonstrated by Louisville's Southern Baptist seminary in dismissing modernistic professors), and unqualified assurances are given that all instruction shall conform strictly to the Brief Statement, etc., or else not a single penny will henceforth be forthcoming from anywhere in Synod. This will produce either a parting of the ways, or a house-cleaning. And there would be nothing unfair or uncharitable about this action. After all, I do not consider any pastor in Synod obliged, year after year, to deliver widows' mites for the support of ambitious Rationalists who spend their time destroying the Christian faith of the widows' sons and daughters! Needless to say, this is not a blanket condemnation of everyone at Valparaiso.

Then there is the element of honesty which has long troubled me in this connection: Valparaiso knows of course that it does not represent the historical doctrinal position of Synod. It also knows that it is this historic position which Synod's laypeople think of when they hear the terms "God's Word," "Lutheran doctrine," "Lutheran Confessions," and the like. Yet Valparaiso does not hesitate, in its appeals for funds, to describe itself as a great Lutheran University, loyal to the Bible and to the Lutheran Confessions, a veritable bulwark of the Faith in our confused age, etc.! Is this quite honest? Again, when laypeople read, in Synod's organ, their President's thoroughly Scriptural, Lutheran sermons at Valparaiso, coupled with official endorsements of the University, what can they conclude but that their venerable President's firm position is what Valparaiso stands for and teaches to its students? After all, those laymen can't see the derisive sneers with which those splendid Presidential sermons are greeted in some quarters! Is this fair to our laity?

Of course, no one is consciously being dishonest. No one in particular is responsible. Boards and committees are not persons and are in a sense amoral. Yet all of us, as our society in general, seem to be caught in an inexorably impersonal organizationalism, in which, without anyone's conscious intention, the budget rules, truth must yield to pragmatism, stalemate must be called "peace," and, in general, almost anything is permissible — except the unforgivable sin against the Organization, that of revealing the truth to the public! Someday this whole structure of make-believe will collapse, and the longer we wait, the greater the pressures that build up, the greater the force of the ultimate explosion.

Needless to say, this goes far beyond the mere question of Valparaiso. We are dealing with the cancer which has long ago destroyed the vitals of American Protestantism and reduced it to an undignified farce. That same cancer, pragmatism, is now gnawing at the heart of a Confessional Lutheranism that has grown rich and ambitious. It is this lethal pragmatism which demands that "for the sake of peace," "blood-bought souls," " the Kingdom," etc., the real state of affairs in the Church be hidden from the gaze of the laity, and, if possible, from the ministry. I am becoming convinced, by daily contact, that vast numbers of fairly intelligent Christian laymen have never heard about Modernism, haven't the slightest inkling of the fact that their own denomination has long ago been destroyed by this evil, and wouldn't recognize a modernist if they saw one! As in the days of St. John Chrysostom, "the ears of the people are holier than the mouths of the priests!"

What can be done to preserve Synod from such a dreadful fate? The danger signals are there: Pastors are ill-informed, unaware of the true state of affairs in world Lutheranism. Unable to cope with the subtle, insidious form of modern pietistic Rationalism. How much more so the laity! For years they have been "shielded" from the whole inter-synodical mess, while their pastors have increasingly abdicated doctrinal responsibilities to professional theologians. Who is prepared to do real battle?

Who is willing to go beyond words to action, to risk pension, parsonage, friends, etc.? Thank God, many watchmen on Zion's walls still remain awake and ready. But, in general, would many be willing to stand alone, especially if it meant standing against a Synodical administration, should it ever happen that liberals should seize control?

At San Francisco, Dr. Behnken, I was one of those who hoped, yes, I'm not ashamed to confess, even prayed for your re-election. And I was moved beyond words by your touchingly beautiful, simple, humble speech of acceptance. It was a moment of true greatness and nobility, the kind that incited in me deep moral shame for ever having uttered or thought a word against you.

Yet Lutheranism's victory at San Francisco, unless its advantages are at once exploited, will be dissipated by the time of the next Convention when the combination of a satisfied, secure, even apologetic conservatism and a dissatisfied, scheming, aggressive liberalism may well issue in doctrinal reversals and in the election of a liberal, or worse, a pietistically anti-theological Praesidium, beneath whose benevolently dozing eyes liberalism may proceed to exterminate the last vestiges of confessional integrity, all "for the Kingdom" and "for souls," of course.

I know very well that the burdens of your office are heavy and sour, as were the duties of Moses and Aaron, Jeremiah and Isaiah and Elijah, Peter and Paul, Athanasius and Augustine, Luther and Walther. I wouldn't write to you merely to annoy you with yet more demands to claim your attention. Rather, I write to make a specific petition for specific action, which, I believe, God will bless. What I seek is some way to end the terrific buildup of pressure regarding the true state of affairs. The danger of the neo-orthodoxy heresy, in itself, is not very great. The cloak of secrecy is what produces those pressure buildups, composed of theological forces and counterforces, seeking expression for which official channels are not providing, and complicated by rumors and suspicions, subterfuges and insinuations, fears and frustrations. So long as "the lid stays on," these pressures must continue to build up until they become intolerable. Now what would happen if the "lid" were removed, if Synodical officials, in a calm, orderly way, gave a detailed, honest report of the state of affairs to its clergy, and appointed trial committees to purify, first of all, the Seminaries? If the truth came out, no matter how shocking, Synod would not be shaken. There would be no stampede, no explosion. The pressures would be dissipated by a thorough, systematic airing. Synod's core, thank God, is still healthy enough. As soon as the cancer is revealed officially, Synod will support official surgery, even if it would mean a loss of 20 per cent, or more. After this painful convulsion, Synod would be healthier, stronger, happier, and united. We would be free as "brethren to dwell together in unity," forgetting personal animosities, to turn jointly to the rebuilding and enlarging of Zion's walls, "with malice toward none and charity toward all."

But if current pressures are allowed to build up further, there is no telling what might happen. If the Praesidium does not find ways very shortly to relieve these tensions, by bringing everything out into the open, where it can be dealt with in the light of day, private efforts, with the best intentions, will produce an explosion which will probably not purify Synod but split it into fragments. Only a firm *officially* instituted disciplinary procedure can hope to receive the backing of a Synod accustomed to official leadership. Disastrous as private action would be, it would become necessary if officials do not implement St. Bernard's truly Christian maxim: "It is better that a scandal should arise than the truth should be surrendered!" And, thank God, our Synod, with all its faults, is not the corrupt machine St. Bernard was facing. If our officials give us bold leadership, chancing Synod's temporal advantages if need be, Synod would follow faithfully through storm and tempest. It wouldn't be the first time in Church or Synodical history. God Himself would support our leaders and give them victory over His enemies, witting and unwitting.

I am not blind enough to believe, with (self-) righteous wrath, that our troubles are undeserved. Dr. Graebner, with all his mistakes, was profoundly right in warning that a certain myopic legalism would produce a terrible liberal reaction. It has! And we conservatives have not always, even when we wanted to, served the Church's best interests, or acted with the greatest wisdom or love. But lest you should think that I am confessing other people's sins, let me say that I feel personally addressed — though all historical analogies are more or less faulty — by St. Asthanasius' own defense of St. Basil, who had been accused of compromising. The passage, which my source gives in German (Boehringer), does apply to the relation of concerned conservatives to their orthodox, prudent, evangelical leaders. Writes St. Athanasius:

> die Moenche sollen als Soehne ihrem Vater, dem Bischof, gehorchen. Waere er verdaechtig, so wuerden sie sich ihm mit Recht widersetzen. Wenn sie aber versichert sein koennen, wie wir denn dessen alle gewiss sind, dass er der Ruhm der Kirche ist, ein Kaempfer fuer die Wahrheit und Lehrer der Beduerftigen, so muss man gegen einen solchen Mann nicht kaempfen, sondern ihn vielmehr anerkennen. Er ist, wie ich dessen fest ueberzeuget bin, den Schwachen schwach geworden, damit er die Schwachen gewinne. Darum sollen sie sein Ziel, welches die Wahrheit ist, und sein kluges Benehmen unter den obwaltenden Umstaenden anerkennen und den Herrn preisen, dass er einen solchen Bischof Kappadozien gegeben hat, wie er jedem Lande zu wuenschen waere.

May God graciously grant such wisdom and charity to all of us, leaders and followers!

The great Arian controversy is analogous to our situation in more ways than one. Then too the very essence of Christ's holy religion was at stake. Then too naïve "peace-makers" claimed that it was all a matter of words, that unscriptural expressions like *homoousios* should not be "forced" on anyone, that both sides ought to "return" to simple "Scriptural" formulae, which Arians also could accept, that Arians and Catholics should form a united front against paganism, etc.

You, Dr. Behnken, indeed have no need to be instructed in history or theology by me, and it would be highly arrogant of me to offer these remarks in this sense. But just as the Absolution is spoken not to inform but to comfort, so these remarks are intended as a small voice of cheer and support for a father in Christ whose lot it is to bear the burden of history, to hold in his hands the fate of a part of Christ's Church in a time of confusion: Just as the Lord of the Church blessed and supported His confessors in the Arian controversy, even against "impossible" odds, even when all seemed lost and the Empire itself was arrayed against the Faith, so also He will give victory to the leaders of His people today, who dare to face the seemingly insuperable inundations of heresy, and to do this, like Gideon, without reliance on human devices, without regard to strategic probabilities, in blind obedience to and trust in the sheer majesty of the divine Word.

By God's providence you hold in your hands, though not for long, the power to save or destroy, humanly speaking, if not the Lutheran Church, at least the Missouri Synod. How easily, once, during the Crypto-Calvinistic conspiracy at Wittenberg, could the well-meaning, orthodox Elector August, completely against his wishes, have become, before the inexorable verdict of history and of history's Lord, the destroyer of the Lutheran Church (again humanly speaking)! Yet, owing to his resolute removal of the conspirators, after the conspiracy had been providentially revealed, the Elector has gone down in history as the divinely-chosen "savior" of the Lutheran Church! How dearly I wish that this honor should come upon you, with respect to our beloved little Lutheran Zion! Not for your sake, or mine, of course, but for the sake of Christ's one, holy, catholic, and apostolic Church, the ground and pillar of truth, which we confess in the Creed, which is the Mother of us all and of all Christians, and which has declared her pure, eternal, unchangeable Faith in our precious Lutheran Confessions!

Forgive me, if all this seems bold and wanting in propriety. I dare to speak thus only because I cannot but sense the desperateness of the situation. And by flattery, which is contrary to charity and to the Eighth Commandment, I could serve neither you nor Christ.

Kurt Marquart

From Part III "What Is Troubling the Lutherans?"
June 1962, by Herman Otten, Church League of America

1. _____ is but an aspect of a much larger situation.
2. Valparaiso is no longer _____.
3. Valparaiso University, barring a miracle, was lost for the _____.
4. An LCMS pastor should not be obliged to deliver "widows mites" to support _____.
5. What is the unforgivable sin against the Organization _____.
6. Vast numbers of fairly intelligent laymen have never heard of _____.
7. Pastors are uninformed about _____.
8. What is worse than the election of a liberal Praesidium? _____
9. The cloak of secrecy produces _____.
10. Synodical officials should give a detailed honest report of _____.
11. After a painful convulsion, the LCMS would be _____.
12. A certain myopic legalism produces _____.
13. Elector August went down in history as the divinely chosen "savior" of the Lutheran Church because _____.
14. "I dare to speak this because I cannot but sense the _____."

THE CRISIS IN CHRISTENDOM

One hundred years ago there occurred a great crisis in American Lutheranism: Influential men in the Eastern synods openly declared war on the distinctive doctrines of the Lutheran Church. The Augsburg Confession was viewed as an outmoded European document, and a Romanizing one at that, which was to be corrected to fit the American situation. This "correction" meant the elimination of those doctrines which had separated Lutherans and Reformed for four hundred years. In other words, the Lutheran Church was to make its peace with "American Evangelical Protestantism," that is, join Reformed sectarianism. Doctrinally it meant unconditional surrender. By the grace of God this surrender did not take place. The "American Recension of the Augsburg Confession", as it was called, received the dishonorable burial it deserved and the confessional synods of the Midwest succeeded in gaining well-nigh universal recognition, at least in theory, for the normative character of the Lutheran Symbols in the Lutheran Church.

Today, a century later, the Church faces another theological crisis, this time an incomparably graver one. Today's crisis is at once more radical and more subtle than the previous one. If the distinctive doctrines of Lutheran Church were at stake then, it is the distinctive doctrines of Christianity itself which are at stake today. The Scripture was attacked indirectly, through the Lutheran Symbols; today, Scripture is attacked directly. Then it was particular doctrines which were denied; today it is all doctrine, the very concept of doctrine. No longer is it this or that aspect of revelation which is questioned, but all revelation, and the very idea of revelation. Not this or that particular truth is rejected, but all truth, and the very possibility of truth. Herein lies the intensive, vertical radicalism of the current crisis. Extensively, horizontally, the crisis is equally radical: the conflict is and must be fought on a global scale, owing to the great advances in transportation and communication and the resultant "ecumenical" developments. The front cuts across most Synodical and denominational lines. The conflict is a total one, as can be expected in an age of total conflicts, when the world is split into two camps, one representing Western civilization with all its virtues and vices, and the other, that Satanically virile monolithic monster of systematized barbarity, Communism. As the political conflict in our time is irreconcilable, radical, and total, both ideologically and geographically, so, equally, is the ecclesiastical-theological one, only more so; for the latter involves the dimension of eternity as no merely political war ever could.

I. THE MODERN CLAIM STATED

The impression may prevail here and there that the main issue in the current controversy about the Word of God is the doctrine of the Inerrancy or Infallibility of the Sacred Scriptures, while all that involved and confusing talk about truth and revelation may be safely left to the experts. Denial of inerrancy is, of course, bad enough. But in this case the inerrancy as such is a relatively subsidiary issue. The real issue has to do with the very concept of truth and revelation.

We could put the question this way: "What is Truth?" But this would be misleading. It would tend to confirm the soothing idea that the question is really only one about the meaning of certain words. Taken this way, it all looks so harmless: Learned gentlemen, using a highly technical jargon, are conducting an interminable professional discussion among themselves on how the word "truth" is used by St. Paul, St. John, the Old Testament, etc. There are formidably numerous references to concordances, and perhaps now and then some mention of Plato or Aristotle. In short, as far as the Christian public is concerned, it all looks like a most wholesome endeavor to "take seriously", as we say nowadays, the "Biblical" meanings of words, which, alas, have become overlaid with Aristotelian-scholastic encrustations. If only these barnacles, for which the "dogmaticians" are blamed, could be removed, so goes the argument, then the Gospel would again shine forth in all its full-orbed Biblical radiance and power—realities which, one must admit, are not too evident in the disoriented, undisciplined chaos which is modern Protestantism. Well, what can be the harm in all this? Why should we not go back to the Biblical ways of thinking and speaking? And in any case, even if some mistakes are made, even if some words are not defined quite exactly, what of it? What if a few verbal tags are misplaced, so long as the things themselves remain what they are? Ah, but they don't! What is the point? That is why the question should be not: "What is Truth?" but: "Is there Truth at all?"

Writing in the *Christian Century,* mouthpiece of religious liberalism in America, a Mr. T. A. Gill analyses the Lutheran Free Conference held in Minneapolis in 1954, and in this connection says some things which are typical of practically the whole of post-Barthian theology. Mr. Gill quotes the principle cited in the Smalcald Articles: "The Word of God shall establish articles of faith, and no one else, not even an angel." But then he adds the extraordinary interpretation: "In the above quotation it is not the Bible but Jesus Christ who establishes articles of faith."[1]

On this-basis, Mr. Gill entertains ecumenical hopes for the Lutheran Church: "If Lutherans will just start to be Lutherans at this point,... When with their beloved Martin they let loose of the propositional nature of God's revelation and take a chance on its personal communication in Christ. . . ."

Notice the basic claim, succinctly stated: Not the Bible, but Christ is authoritative. Revelation is not propositional. This can only mean that there is no such thing as divinely revealed, authoritative, final doctrine, *doctrina divina.* Let us pursue this central theme in the writings of several representative modern theologians.

Emil Brunner, a major figure in the new (Barthian) school, writes:

> The fundamental error, which identifies Revelation and revealed doctrine, begins with the apologists, but it has its roots already in the Pastoral Epistles and in the Apostolic Fathers (cf. Titus 2:10,

and the whole valuation of "sound doctrine").[2] ...but because he himself is the Word, and is therefore never dissolved into human words, therefore no doctrinal formation, no matter how good, can claim to be God's Word itself, or even only the "right" doctrine, finished and infallible, once and for all.[3]

In the Reformation's understanding, however, as in the Bible itself, not doctrine but Jesus Christ Himself is the object of faith. Doctrine is only a ministering medium, only a grasping (Fassung), and therefore never infallible. Therefore, faith has not to do with doctrine, but with the subject, or rather the Person meant by it. Doctrine is only a pointer, even though it be an unequivocal, appropriate pointer. Therefore faith does not cling to doctrine, but glides along it, toward the target, like a bullet in a rifle. Doctrine is the telescope, through which we are to see Him Himself. Thus doctrine is never the object of faith, but it is expression, confession of faith. In a Confession the Church expresses her faith, but she does not prescribe her confession to the individual, as that which is to be believed. . .

. . . right doctrine. What does that mean? It means first of all: doctrine which corresponds to Biblical, apostolic doctrine. But with that the problem of right doctrine is not solved, but merely postponed. For even within the Bible itself the problem of right doctrine reappears. We have already seen that in the Bible itself an unqualified unity of doctrine is not to be found, but only a convergence of modes of teaching upon a common center. "Right" doctrine, then, will have to be understood literally as "right-directed", correctly aimed doctrine, never in the sense of an identity of concept and the subject matter meant by it, but always only in the sense of a definite, unequivocal pointer. Not a system of finished mechanically coordinated (nebeneinander stehender) doctrines, but only doctrine as pointers radically aiming at a center, corresponds to the Word of God, which He himself, the Son of God, is, and in which He himself personally communicates himself in address (Andrede).

The correctness of theological doctrines and concepts is determined by their directions, by the unequivocal manner in which they point Him out. There is no closed theological system of doctrine; the ideal of the scholastic *summa theologiae* is a phantom.[4]

Other spokesman say the same thing:

From a very early time in the history of the Church the tendency had manifested itself to equate divine revelation with a body of information which God has communicated to man. . .Behind this tendency lay a strong sense of the necessity of preserving unity of doctrine throughout the Church — in other words, a growing necessity of *orthe doxa,* right opinion, orthodoxy. A beginning of it can already be detected in the latest books of the New Testament itself, but it appears much more plainly in the generation following, and then grow apace.[5]

In the Christian Church the subject matter of revelation has frequently been conceived as infallible doctrine, which in turn is thought of as a series of propositions which can be supported by the citation of numerous proof-texts from the Bible. In this sense the Bible has been as a source of revealed doctrine. It is dear, however, that the Bible does not present us with doctrine of this type...[6]

As for Karl Barth himself, Dr. Robert Preus of St. Louis, in an extended study comes to the conclusion that,

One of the most dangerous elements in neo-orthodoxy's doctrine of revelation is the denial of the dianoetic nature and purpose of revelation, that revelation is addressed among things to man's intellectual capacity and is received also by the intellect.[7]

And Dr. Preus sees clearly that Barth is no exception. He too, denies the existence of revealed doctrine or propositional truth.

Anders Nygren and Gustaf Aulen, the foremost "Lutheran" representatives of neo-orthodoxy, though they differ from Barth on even some basic definitions, are, if anything, even more vehemently opposed to the idea of propositional, revealed truth or doctrine. Aulen rejects what he calls "the confusion of divine revelation with some given, authoritative theological system of doctrine."[8] And he insists that "the affirmations of faith are, without exception, of a symbolic character."[9] The affirmations of faith have no revelation to theoretical knowledge or metaphysics. In other words, they do not contain real, propositional truth or knowledge. The distinction between the symbolic affirmations of faith and real or theoretical knowledge is quite evident also in Nygren, who places "religious statements" besides and therefore outside the realm of the theoretical, that is, propositional truth or knowledge. The affirmations of faith, then, are not "true" or "false"; they are simply "religious".[10]

The whole situation is neatly summed up in the German title of one of Brunner's books, *Wahrheit als Begegnung: Truth as Encounter.*

It is clear from the preceding that infinitely more that philology (e. g. the meaning of the word "truth") is at stake. Modern theology does not claim that while there is true, revealed doctrine, this should not be called truth. The claim is rather that in the traditional sense, as propositions, truth as revealed doctrine *does not exist.* And as the fox, when he saw that he could not reach the grapes, decided that they were sour and therefore, after all, not desirable, so modern theology, having rejected all external religious authority, and finding it impossible to arrive at any sort of stable, substantive doctrinal convictions, heaps upon the traditional concept of revealed propositional truth all sorts of ill-deserved abuse ("Scientific", "materialistic", "Greek", "Aristotelian", "Scholastic", "rationalistic", "impersonal", "static", etc.)

But if there is no truth, then theology and the Church are out of business. If one wishes to remain "in business", one must continue to speak about "truth". And so the word is simply taken and "redefined" to mean something altogether different. It now becomes either Christ Himself, or God's faithfulness, or the "divine-human" encounter — anything except its proper propositional meaning.

It is clear that this notion of "Truth" and "Revelation" and the corre-

37

sponding notion of "Faith", are entirely subjectivistic and enthusiastic ("Schwaermerisch") since the dianoetic, doctrinal element is, by definition, totally absent.

That all this amounts to unrelieved skepticism should be evident:

. . . the utter skepticism of this position, in which not only verbal symbols but the conceptual content itself is not what God really wills to give us, is disclosed in pious phrases about a personal truth, or Du-Wahrheit, distinct from the subject-predicate relation called Es-Wahrheit. God cannot be an object of thought He cannot be a Gegenstand for the human mind. Truth, instead of being a matter of propositions, is a personal encounter. Whatever words God might speak, Brunner not only reduces to hints or pointers, but also holds that God's words may be false. "God can, if he wishes, speak his word to man even through false doctrine." This is the culmination, and comment should be superfluous.[11]

. . . Barth thinks that no religious truth is accessible to us: God is unknown. He is *Deus absconditus*, the hidden God. According to Barth, no truth about God exists...

. . . As I have shown in my chapter on Aulen (below, p. 188f.) the Lundensian Theology, like Barthianism, represents a real nihilism in regard to truth.[12]

II. THE MODERN CLAIM EXAMINED

Gordon H. Clark observes rather penetrating:

. . . If there could be a truth inexpressible in logical, grammatical form, the word *truth* as applied to it would have no more in common with the usual meaning of truth than the Dog star has in common with Fido . . . Certainly, the burden of proof lies on those who deny the propositional construction of truth. Their burden is two-fold. Not only must they give evidence for the existence of such truth, but first of all they must make clear what they mean by their words. It may be that the phrase non-propositional *truth* is a phrase without meaning . . . Carnell illustrates the first species of truth by saying: "The trees in the yard are truly trees." No doubt they are, but this does not convince one that a tree is a truth. To say that the trees are truly trees is merely to put literary emphasis on the proposition, the trees are trees... In such illustrations no truth is found that is not propositional and no evidence for two species of truth is provided. Carnell then describes a student taking an examination in ethics. The student may know the answers, even though he himself is not moral. But the student's mother wants him not so much to know the truth as to be the truth. Carnell insists that the student can be the truth. Now, obviously the mother wants her son to be moral, but what meaning can be attached to the phrase that the mother wants her son to be the truth? Let it be that thinking is only preparatory to being moral, as Carnell says, but what can be meant by being the truth, i.e., what more can be meant than being moral? The student could not be a tree.[13]

38

To avoid a lot of useless and irrelevant philology. The issue must be properly defined. The question is not whether "loyalty", "faithfulness", etc. occur, especially in the Old Testament, as proper meanings of the term "truth", (Emeth, emunah, qoshet, aletheia.) That is cheerfully granted. The question is: Is the idea of propositional truth and revelation inculcated by the Scriptures? Or is the denial of propositional truth in harmony with Biblical thought-forms? Does the orthodox position rest on philosophy?

Propositional Truth in Scripture

Is it really true that "in no instance does it (truth in the Bible, K. M.) signify factual precision, as truth is usually understood today"?[14] (It should be noted here that if "factual precision" is to define truth as it "is usually understood today", precision must mean correctness, not exactness. For example: "Queen Victoria died in the twentieth century" is a correct, and therefore completely true statement, and it is exact enough for some purposes, i.e. in terms of centuries. But in terms of decades, years, months, days, hours, or minutes, the statement is increasingly inexact. Truth, even today, always means correctness, not necessarily exactness.)

Since the "Johannine concept" of truth is supposed to be particularly mystical, let us begin with an example from the Fourth Evangelist, St. John 4, 18. To the Samaritan woman, who said, "I have no husband," our Lord replied that since she had had five husbands and since her present consort was not her husband, her answer was quite correct: "In that saidst thou truly." Obviously Christ means "factual precision." Certainly He is not attributing "faithfulness", "loyalty", etc., to the woman! One further aspect should be noted. Christ tells the woman that she had had five husbands. Are we to assume that perhaps the women actually had had nine husbands, or two, or seven, but that neither she nor Christ nor the Evangelist saw any difficulty in stating the number as five, since none of the persons involved wished to "satisfy a modern statistician", and since, in any case, "a concern for the truth in the sense of factual accuracy is a phenomenon peculiar to Western culture"?[15]

Of another woman we read in St. Mark 5:33 that she came to Christ and "told him all the truth." Again this can only mean "factual precision". Certainly she is not preaching the Gospel to our Lord! She simply narrated the prosaic facts of her case, which were "existential" enough, to be sure, but certainly not particularly "Christocentric", as all "Biblical truth" is supposed to be! And in practice we find that the Bible is full of instances of truth which cannot possibly be "Biblical" in the sense of neological theory. Gen. 42:16; Deut. 22:20; 2 Sam. 7:28; Prov. 22:21; Psalm 15, 2; St. John 8:14, 17, 44-46; 10:41; 19:35; Acts 26:25 2 Cor. 7:14; 12:6; 1 Tim. 2:7; 2 Tim. 2:18; 4:4; Tit. 1:13; Eph. 4:25; etc.

Aside from the use of the word, we have, already in the Old Testament, clear instances of the concept of a revealed body of dogma and law, to be transmissively and authoritatively taught, Deut. 11:18ff; 29:29; Is. 8:20; Ps. 106:12; Ps. 119. Liberals usually admit this, but then disavow it contemptuously: "Cornill has shown that with the solemn reception of Deuteronomy the book religion was born. We add: the legalistic book-religion."[16]

Emil Brunner also belittles this mere "Old Testament level of revelation."[17]

As a matter of fact we find the same insistence on propositional, dogmatic revelation in the New Testament. Consider the *"logia tou theou"* of Romans 3:2, or St. Paul's inculcation of "sound doctrine" in the Pastorals, or the "book religion" of 2 Tim. 3:16, or that same holy Apostle's confession: "believing all things which are written in the law and in the prophets" (Acts 24:14). Above all, Christ Himself teaches us to treat Scripture as absolutely authoritative: "Scripture cannot be broken." (St. John 10:35). It should be noted that the reference is to a specific proposition, even one of the apparent insignificance. Yet, even that proposition "cannot be broken", simply because it is Scripture, not because it has this or that beneficial effect on anyone! And when our Lord refutes the Sadducees, St. Matthew 22:23ff., He (1) identifies error with definite propositions, not encounters, (2) opposes to them other propositions, and (3) establishes the truth in the matter not even with a direct proposition from Scripture, but with a mere *deduction* - suspiciously Aristotelian - from Scriptural propositions!

> Only in an age like ours, when words have been taken out of their living texture of men's morally responsible lives, . . . only in such an age is it conceivable that theologians should grow coy and bemused about *verba*. Since it takes words seriously, the Bible has no romantic aversion to the book as such. One can hardly imagine the Apostles getting "excited" over the reproach that theirs is a "book-religion."[18]

But Brunner and the moderns do not hesitate to impute error even to the New Testament. We have seen before that Brunner traces what he calls "the fundamental error, which identifies Revelation and revealed doctrine" to the New Testament, namely, the Pastoral Epistles. On the very next page he repeats the attack, again in a footnote: "The word of the 2nd Epistle to Timothy, 'all divinely inspired Scripture is profitable for doctrine,' (3, 16), which, falsely translated, became the *locus classicus* of the doctrine of Verbal inspiration, *betrays the beginning of this disastrous identification."* [19] (Our emphasis)

John Baillie, as we have seen, also wishes to correct Scripture. Recall his statement, quoted above, concerning "the tendency... to equate divine revelation with a body of information"; *"A beginning of it can already be detected in the latest books of the New Testament itself."*

It is necessary to call attention to these disavowals because popularizers of the Brunner-Baillie ideas in hitherto conservative denominations cannot—yet!—afford to go quite that far without jeopardizing their whole mission. But their caution should not blind us to the nature of the ultimate destination!

Not to be overlooked in this discussion are the many Scriptures texts which teach or imply the dogmatic, dianoetic content of Christian faith, the fact that there must be *fides quae* before there can be *fides qua,* a belief *that,* not merely belief in Ps. 106:12; St. Matt. 16:13ff.; St. John 2:22; 5:4647 ; 20:31; Acts 24:14; Heb. 11:1ff. While faith is *more* than assent, it is not *less,* Romans 10:14ff; 1 Cor. 14:7ff.

We cannot conclude this section without referring to St. John 14:6: "I am the Way, the Truth, and the Life." Does this mean that the "Biblical concept" of truth is "personal" (Christ Himself), rather than propositional?

It should be quite evident that this text tells us not what way, truth and life mean, but Who Christ is. Unless the words already had clear meanings in the minds of the hearers, Christ's application of them to Himself would have been totally meaningless. These words, and others like them (door, bread, water, resurrection, etc.) have figurative, not literal meanings when applied to Christ. They should be capitalized, for they have become "new words", as Luther proves to the Zwinglians in a similar case (St. Louis ed., XX:905 ff; quoted in Pieper's *Dogmatics, III,* 307).

It would be absurd to argue that the "Biblical concept" of "door", "way", "water", etc. are not "wooden", "stone", and "wet", respectively, but "personal." Why then, should "truth", of all words, be subjected to such nonsense?

Now Who it Philosophizing?

It is often implied and stated that the orthodox view of revelation is based on (antiquated) philosophy, while the modern, anti-propositional view is "Biblical". That at least the latter is not the case we have already shown. It remains to see in what way and on which side philosophy is involved.

To suggest that the orthodox concept of authoritative propositional truth, dogma, is "Greek," while the pietistically sugar-coated agnosticism of the modern, tentative sore of "theology" is "Biblical," it to turn the facts topsy-turvy and to betray a total lack of perspective. Exactly the opposite is the case! It is precisely Biblical religion which insists on the absolute and universal significance of historically-anchored particularities.

The religion of the Incarnation proposes to men divine truth, not an eternal quest for it. Not by human achievement, but by divine condescension, truth is available, here and now, Deuteronomy 30:11-14; Romans 10:6-8. Obedience and faithfulness to the known truth, not search for the unknown, is the basic characteristic of Biblical religion and one cannot obey what one has not yet found!

To all of this speculative, anti-dogmatic temper of ancient Greece is diametrically opposed. The Bible *has* truth; the Greeks *seek* it. Anti-Christian authors put it rather bluntly:

> The Greeks had no authoritative Sacred Book, no creed, no ten commandments, no dogmas. The very idea of orthodoxy was unknown to them. They had no theologians to draw up sacrosanct definitions of the eternal and infinite. They never tried to define it; only to express or suggest it.[20] J. B. S. Haldane counts fanaticism among the only really important inventions made between 3000 B. C. and 1400

A. D. It was a Judaic-Christian invention.[21] On p. 82 the concept of fanaticism is specified: "uncompromising, intolerant, proclaiming the one and only truth.")

By the same token the concept of divinely revealed doctrine is certainly anything but "Aristotelianism" remains to be demonstrated. But if that charge refers simply to the use of logic, it should be pointed out that Aristotle did not invent logic, but merely described some aspects of it. The essentials of logic presupposed in any intelligible human discourse, and Scripture is no exception:

> With reference to logical forms our Lord used *analogy,* Luke 11, 13; *reduction ad adsurdum.* Matt. 12:26; *excluded middle,* Matt. 12:30; a *fortiori,* Matt. 12: 1-8; *Implication,* Matt. 12: 28; and the law of *non-contradiction,* Luke 6:39.[22]

If orthodoxy is "Aristotelian" at this point, then so is Scripture - and Plato!

But if the philosophical shoe does not fit the orthodox foot, it fits the neo-orthodox one perfectly. "The modern notion that any human word is necessarily a distortion of the divine revelation which it mediates is not shared by the apostles and prophets."[23] But if this "modern notion" does not come from Scripture, where does it come from? It is a strictly philosophical assumption, an epistemological extension of the Old Calvinistic heresy: *Finitum non capax infiniti.* "Barth and neo-orthodoxy are still unable to emancipate themselves from that old saw," comments Dr. Robert Preus.[24]

And the "old saw" has a very ancient and respectable philosophical name: Platonism!

Bengt Haegglund has shown that the entire modern understanding of Scripture is based on essentially Platonic premises. Whereas Aristotelianism regards words as adequate vehicles of meaning, refusing to seperate word (signum) and meaning (signatum) in such a way as to render the latter "an independent area, which is only partially attainable through the words,"[25] Platonism regards words as symbols or pointers which can only hint at realities which always remain transcendent and ultimately inexpressible. The modern notion of Scripture, which separates revelation from the word of Scripture, the divine Word from the human words of the Bible, merely echoes the Platonic separation of *signum* and *signatum.* The whole perspective is determined *a priori* by the Platonic notion that ultimate truth is eternally transcendent and therefore can be conveyed only imperfectly and indirectly by human words. Unlike the Bible (1 Tim. 4:7; 2 Tim. 4:4; Tit. 1:14; 2 Pet. 1:16), both Plato and modern theology resort to myth to express the inexpressible.

The concept of myth is directly related to an even more specific involvement of modern theology in philosophy. Barthianism speaks of two kinds of events. The one kind takes place in ordinary human experience and history. These are factual or historical events. But then there is "Urgeschichte," primal history (here enter "true" myth, legend, or epic), or faith history, etc., and it is in this "plane of faith" that revelation takes place. Even the Resurrection is, for Brunner, not a historical event, observable in principle by anyone, but a "faith-event," or a "kingdom-event," perceptible only to faith.[26] Comments Jewitt: "The prosaic mind can hardly escape the suspicion that an event which did not happen in time and space, did not happen at all."[27] And Olav Valen Sendstad concludes:

> The entire Barthian neo-orthodoxy and incarnation teaching opens out in the idealistic and mystic banality that God's self-disclosure takes place in the hidden, unknowable sphere of the "I", *not* history, not in the psychophysical world which now at this time is our world.[28]

It is not difficult to recognize Kant's distinction between phenomena and things-in-themselves behind the theological distinction between ordinary events and "faith-events." Willis B. Grover, who asserts a "debilitating Kantian basis" for current Protestant theology, writes, in a journal which can hardly be accused of orthodox bias:

> In his book *Resurrection and Historical Reason* (Scribner's 1957), Professor (Richard R.) Niebuhr denies that the so-called neo-orthodoxy of recent decades marks a fundamental break with the theological method of the 19th century. Schleiermacher and Feuerbach, Barth, Brunner and Bultmann are *variations of one Kantian theme.* Mr. Niebuhr perhaps does not sufficiently recognize the very real differences between those variations, but his study is limited to the question of theological method, and *his contention that Kant's distinction between the phenomenal and the noumenal is basic to the thought of the most influential Protestant theologian of the last century and a half can hardly be questioned.*[29] (Our emphasis)

Under "Hermeneutics" in Section III we shall have to take up the problem of philosophy again. Here it is sufficient to sketch Neo-Orthodoxy's deep and fatal philosophical involvements. When Neo-Orthodoxy cries "Aristotelianism!" at the mere sight of anything definite, we need only consider the source: The allergic reaction is natural for a perspective informed by Platonic mysticism and Kantian critical philosophy, not to mention Existentialist subjectivism!

"Neo-Orthodoxy" Or "Crypto-Liberalism"?

Neo-Orthodoxy, rather fittingly, constitutes a paradox: On the one hand it is an improvement on the old Liberalism, and on the other hand it is a "new and worse form of modernism."[30]

It cannot be denied that the advent of Karl Barth has meant a change for the better in fashionable theological circles. The great historic terms of Christian doctrine became respectable again. Scripture came to be viewed as somehow theologically authoritative again, even though that authority proved to be chronically theoretical. But it was a vast improvement over the Liberal approach, which regarded the Bible as religious literature only, a mere product of human evolution. At least men were *trying* to find God's Word and revelation again!

Upon closer inspection, however, one finds that Barthianism could offer penetrating, even brilliant diagnoses, but few, if any, cures. Philo-

43

sophical pessimism replaced philosophical optimism. Particular developments of Liberalism were attacked, but Liberalism itself could not be overcome. For all its criticism, Barthianism was but Liberalism's own reaction to its own excesses. With respect to the fundamental issue of the authority of Scripture, Barthianism never stepped outside the well-marked boundaries of Liberal assumptions. The whole critical approach to Scripture was taken over *in toto* by Barthianism. For Barth the Bible is "all the way through fallible human words . . . The fallibility of the Bible, that is to say its liability to mistakes also covers its *religious,* that is its *theological* contents."[31] The prophets and apostles *"could* err, and they *have* also erred in every word . . . but precisely with this *fallible* and *erring* human word they have spoken the word of God."[32] Brunner agrees.[33] He accepts the radical conclusions of Higher Criticism even in the New Testament accounts of the Resurrection of Christ, insisting that there are contradictions between St. Paul and the Gospels on this point, and that the latter "show the influence of the growth of legend."[34]

At least Liberalism was consistent in rejecting the authority of an erring Bible. Barthianism, with its true-and-false Bible is more than a paradox; it is a self-contradiction, from the orthodox as well as from the Liberal points of view:

> Of course, the liberals do not object at all to neo-orthodoxy's use of the results of destructive criticism, but they attack the Barthians on the ground that for all practical purposes they do not use those results to arrive at their conclusions, for if they did, they could not possibly be Barthians but would have to be liberals . . . Barthianism tries to hold to the truth of what John says and at the same time hold that the Gospel is fictitious. One liberal puts it this way: Barthians hold "that these doctrines have some important element of truth in them but are not true in the form in which they were traditionally accepted, while any attempt to say what *is* true ends in logical incoherence."[35]

Barthianism wants to have its cake and eat it too. It wishes to have the comfort of revelation, but also the freedom of Higher Criticism. It wishes to be both under and over the Bible. Orthodoxy sat in its tree and was happy, though "static". Liberalism cut down the branch (or the tree?), had no place left to sit, and hence became "dynamic," though rather less happy. Neo-Orthodoxy, however, cuts off the branch, but continues to sit on it. Perhaps that is why its positions are so impermanent: Gravity is quickly pulling them down toward Bultmann and even Tillich, who may safely be regarded as Absolute Zero on the theological scale! Chester Tulga describes Neo-Orthodoxy, unkindly perhaps, but hardly unfairly, as a "conglomeration of theological gibberish which always follows the collapse of some tower of Babel. Proud liberalism, building a tower to heaven without God, has fallen into confusion of speech."[36]

Barthianism, then, is not orthodox. Nor is it new. The essential elements of the Barthian concept of revelation (denial of the dogmatic, dianoetic element) are clearly evident in the "Positive" school of 19th century theology, which orthodox Lutherans combatted in no uncertain terms as simply another form of subjectivistic, Schleiermacherian ego-theology.[37] And what familiar and modern sounding phrases, slogans, and arguments one finds in those old discussions! For example, Ihmels argues for a concept of revelation "which sees the essential element not in a communication of doctrine, but in an actual stepping-out-of-one-self (Aussichheraustreten) on the part of God." Kier, in his thesis, writes: "Holy Scripture, even though not inspired as a book, remains for the Christian a doctrine of the history of salvation, memorial of the revelations of God, Word of God through the apostles and prophets for all and to all who dwell on earth . . . Such faith cannot be shattered by the recognition that it did not please God to let his witnesses speak and write with a supernatural inerrancy." Luthardt: ". . .Scripture may be regarded as inerrant only in as much as it is a witness and document of the history of salvation and . . . its value and nature is not changed by errors in historical, geographical, scientific and similar things . . . Scripture may not be regarded as a perfect book, in the external pietistic Reformed sense . . . the false un-Lutheran attitude to Holy Scripture, according to which Scripture, rather than, above all, Christ, is made the foundation and cornerstone of faith, and in fact revelation itself. It (Scripture) is the witness and the crowning conclusion of the history of the mighty acts of God . . . Accordingly also the Inerrancy of Holy Scripture is to be measured as something to be understood and measured according to the actual purpose of Scripture. "Scripture, I say with Volck, is something better than a book without errors." Commenting on the claim that Inerrancy is not a Lutheran but a "pietistic-Reformed" idea, C. F. W. Walther thunders: "Dies ist ein ganz entsetzlicher Betrug, den man dem lutherischen Christenvolke spielt." One final example, quoted in *Lehre und Wehre,* and sharply repudiated: ". . . The yoke of a concept of Inspiration like the Jewish scholastic one of the 17th century. . . We need an improved reorganization and enrichment of the doctrine of the divine inspiration of the Bible, but one which would lead us not away from, but deeper into the healthy theological-scientific awareness. The purified and perfected concept of Inspiration . . . must be such that, fully honoring the mysterious work of the Holy Ghost, room is left for unbiased research into its earthly and historical development and mediation. The Bible is to be confessed fully and entirely as God's Word to men and for men . . . True belief in the Inspiration does not exclude but includes a healthy historical-critical conception of Holy Scripture."

David Hedegard[38] traces the Lundensian position, via Archbishop Nathan Soderblom, to Sabatier's fideism. Fideism distinguishes faith and beliefs. Beliefs and dogmas are only symbolic. Faith is not bound to them.

Not only, however, is Neo-Orthodoxy essentially but another form of Liberalism, closely akin to previous pietistic and inconsistent versions of the latter, but there is a deceptiveness about it which orthodox Lutherans can ignore only at their peril. Even Liberals complain of the new Crypto-Liberalism:

> Today's seminary student is likely to have gained the impression
> that liberal theology has been utterly discredited. (It may not be

45

quite so clear to him that about 85 percent of liberalisms' initial accomplishments and attitudes are taken for granted by his teachers)

. . . It is possible to recognize as one of the perils in the present situation the danger that the vital, creative movement from within liberalism which has been unhappily dubbed 'neo-orthodoxy' may unintentionally issue in a caricature of itself - a sort of spongy orthodoxy or spineless fundamentalism, a Biblicism without guts.

A generation of Protestant ministers may be rising which still enjoys the fruits of liberalism's victories but has forgotten the price of liberty, and which has learned to use the vocabulary of orthodoxy without fully knowing how to distinguish that vocabulary from what has traditionally been considered the real thing.[39]

It is refreshing to learn that the deception is also self-deception, but this does not remove the danger. The new theology uses all the traditional dogmatic terms, but fills them with entirely different meanings. Denials and distortions are called "restatements," "redefinitions," etc. Unless orthodox clergy and people are aware of this, they are an easy prey to the innovators. Regarding Barth, the Lundensian Gustav Wingren observes:

If Barth is permitted to construct his whole system in peace, remove the objective existence of evil, the natural knowledge of God, the rule of law in the World, place the revelation of God through the incarnation in the center, define the Gospel as a word about God's disclosure of himself; if he can do all this, then within this framework he can use the whole vocabulary of the New Testament. He can speak of our sin and guilt, our hostility to God, of demonic character. Everything is here, but it is within the frame of reference of our ignorance, and it is a reality only on the basis of our ontological mistake which makes the nonexistent evil into something that exists. Barth has the ability to a very large degree of being able to employ the language of Scripture in a system that is totally foreign to the Bible.[40]

Gustav Aulen repeatedly and grossly denies the authority of Scripture. Yet he also accepts Scripture as the "only infallible rule of faith and life!"[41]

One of the wildest examples of the current assassination of language comes from the pen of the Church of England's post-Barthian Bishop James A. Pike of San Francisco, U. S. A.:

When Norman Pittenger and I were writing *The Faith of the Church* (a semi-official Episcopal book on doctrine), he did not find reason to accept the historical virgin birth; I thought I did. Our wrestling over the matter – not only a personal wrestling but a wrestling with both theological professors and bishops of our church - resulted in the book's leaving an opening for people like Pittenger. Now I am with him. While neither he nor I would deny the possibility of the miracle, the biblical evidence and the theological implications seem to be in favor of assuming that Joseph was the father of Jesus. We certainly do not deny that "the Holy Spirit hovered" (one translation) nor deny in the least the *doctrine* of the virgin birth, namely the paradox which the myth presents so well: Jesus as part of the historical process and also divine interruption in history - a mighty act of God, indeed the Supreme Mighty Act of God.[42]

How does one deny the fact of the virgin birth, and yet not "deny in the least (!) the *doctrine* of the virgin birth"? The word "doctrine" here obviously means something like "symbolical significance," in other words, a non-doctrinal doctrine!

J. G. Machen's eloquent protest against the unethical deceptiveness of the old liberalism applies with full force today:

> In order to maintain themselves in the evangelical churches and quiet the fears of their conservative associates, the liberals resorted constantly to a double use of language. A young man, for example, has received disquieting reports of the unorthodoxy of a prominent preacher. Interrogating the preacher as to his belief, he receives a reassuring reply. "You may tell everyone," says the liberal preacher in effect, "that I believe that Jesus is God." The inquirer goes away much impressed.
>
> It may be doubted, however, whether the assertion, "I believe that Jesus is God," or the like, on the lips of liberal preachers, is strictly truthful. The liberal preacher attaches indeed a real meaning to the words, and that meaning is very dear to his heart. He really does believe that "Jesus is God." But the trouble is that he attaches to the words a different meaning from that which is attached to them by the simple-minded person to whom he is speaking. He offends, therefore, against the fundamental principle of truthfulness in language. According to that fundamental principle, language is truthful, not when the meaning attached to the words by the speaker, but when the meaning intended to be produced in the mind of the particular person addressed, is in accordance with the facts . . . If the audience is composed of old-fashioned Christians, who have never attached anything but the old meaning to the word "God", then the language is untruthful.[43]

How acute the danger actually is, is hinted at by a Reformed writer.

> (Neo-orthodoxy) is unquestionable the theological system taught in some American seminaries which formerly stood for conservative truth. The danger is that since the terminology of Barthianism and conservatism is the same in many areas, the change in these schools and their graduates is not readily discerned. Too many are too quick to white-wash schools and men who still speak of regeneration, inspiration, the authority of the Word, etc., and too few have investigated what is really meant by those terms. The danger of such is like quicksand.[44]

III. IMPLICATIONS FOR THEOLOGY

It should be self-evident that one cannot accept Scripture, which conveys intelligible content, teachings, propositions, as the inspired, revealed Word and truth of God, and then deny that doctrinal revelation, or revealed doctrine, exists! The two positions, representing Christian Theol-

47

ogy and "Modern Theology" respectively, cancel each other. At this point one should be able to conclude the matter with a hearty Q.E.D. In view of the fact, however, that even some "conservatives" persist in writing and acting as if the concepts and tenets of Modern Theology could be used to "enrich" or even "correct" a too-traditional Orthodoxy, it will be necessary to examine in detail some of the fundamental, determinative assumptions underlying each position, in order to show that the two systems, like matter and anti-matter, cannot be used to supplement each other, in the sense of any significant organic combination. Strictly mechanically, of course, any word-patterns can be strung or stitched together—and this is exactly how superficial technicians imagine themselves to be making the Church and Theology "relevant", "timely", "up-to-date", etc. The result however, is, to mix some metaphors, a split level patchwork, a hybrid monstrosity, incapable-and undeserving—of survival or propagation.

What follows is intended to show that historic Christian Theology and Modern Theology proceed from entirely different assumptions and definitions, so that all subsequent assertions, despite superficial, verbal similarities, belong to entirely dissimilar frames of reference, and therefore convey entirely dissimilar, incompatible substance.

The Formal Principle and Hermeneutics

The Formal Principle of Sacred Theology, that which constitutes, determines, and rules every theological discipline, is the Holy Scripture, the Word of God. Christian Theology has no other authority beside these Scriptures of God. This is known as the *sola Scriptura* (Scripture alone) principle. Since *sola Scriptura* is not a mere slogan, suspended as it were in a doctrinal vacuum, and requiring only loud and frequent repetition, but a real working principle, it must have definite content and meaning, including necessary presuppositions and consequences. Prominent among the presuppositions is the doctrine that Scripture-this applies to the original autographs absolutely, to the copies derivatively-is altogether and entirely, without exception or qualification, the inspired, authoritative inerrant Word of God. In practice this must mean that Scripture cannot at any point be criticized or corrected by any other norm, such as human reason, experience, tradition, science, "faith", etc. Unless *sola Scriptura* means that, it means nothing whatever-it is literally non-sense!

As Dr. F. Pieper shows in the first volume of his soundly Biblical *Christian Dogmatics,* the principle of Scriptural authority absolutely determines everything in Theology. Whatever is not thus determined by Scripture, is not Theology, but human notion, opinion, philosophy, and enthusiasm, *Schwaemerei.* Theology rests entirely on faith, and faith can exist only vis-a-vis the Word of God.

Beyond that, both "faith" and "theology" are pure illusion. In other words, the Formal Principle, *with all its presuppositions, including Inerrancy,* precedes Theology as Euclid's axioms precede his geometry. This priority, of course, is strictly logical, not temporal, and has nothing to do

48

with the *ordo salutis:* how an individual receives faith is quite irrelevant here. It means simply that Theology cannot begin without the Scripture-principle. Any abrogation of the latter, whether *de jure* by explicit repudiation, or *de facto,* by the introduction of material derived from other premises, is "unconstitutional", and therefore totally illicit and invalid as Theology: *Quod non est biblicum, non est theologicum!*

Now, no matter what "Biblical" airs it may give itself, Modern Theology abrogates this Formal Principle, the authority of Scripture, and it does so not merely casually, here and there, but systematically, radically, everywhere, all along the line: its "revelation" is not revelation, its "truth" is not truth, its "Word of God" is not the Word of God, its "inspiration" is not inspiration, its "inerrancy" (where retained) is not inerrancy, and its "interpretation" is not interpretation:

> In recent Protestant theology ... a new conception of revelation has appeared ... According to this view, religious revelation does not consist of propositions about God to be believed; it consists of the confrontation ... What is disclosed in such events is "not truth concerning God, but the living God Himself" ...
>
> Every conception of revelation involves a conception of inspiration. The scholastic conception of revelation has generally been accompanied by the theory of the plenary, verbal inspiration of the Bible. Since God speaks propositionally in the Bible, and God is omniscient, every word of the Bible must be infallibly true. The theory of God-acting-in-events has other implications. Since God confronts us through the meaning of events, any report or comment which powerfully conveys that meaning may be divinely inspired, whether or not it is factually inerrant. The Bible can thus convey a true revelation of God, and its writers can be God's inspired interpreters, while at the same time they are thoroughly human and fallible.[45]

If Scripture is "thoroughly human and fallible", it cannot possibly be the authority, the Formal Principle for Theology. What then is the real authority, the real formal principle for Modern Theology? *The Scientific Method!*

The impression-which has many victims-that "Neo-Orthodoxy" has abandoned the faith-less, critical ("objective", "scientific") approach of liberalism, should be quickly dispelled by a perusal of statements such as the following, taken from a quasi-official neological source:

> Neo-orthodoxy agrees with liberalism that the whole area of spatio-temporal fact and event is the valid object of scientific inquiry, with the result that the hypotheses of science in the area of natural and historical fact are regarded as authoritative . . . Likewise, although the Incarnation has become the central theological doctrine of all neo-orthodoxy, the factual manifestations and explanations of the Incarnation (e.g., the miracles, the Virgin Birth, and the Empty Tomb) have not played such a central role in contemporary theology as they did in "orthodoxy". In other words, to the contemporary thinker theological doctrines are statements containing symbolic rather than literal truth, propositions pointing to the religious di-

49

mensions of events rather than propositions containing factual information about events ... The intricate relation between the historic fact and the religious, "mythical" or symbolical interpretation of the fact remains as an important and as yet unresolved problem for neo-orthodoxy.

Secondly, neo-orthodoxy affirms with liberalism that all of the activities and products of man's religious life (scriptures, creeds, churches) are historically conditioned. From this contemporary theology draws two "liberal" conclusions: (1) these scriptures and institutions can and must be studied historically and critically in order to be properly understood; (2) none of these products of man's religious life is in itself infallible or a direct, unmediated result of divine activity.[46]

Whether "theology" be frankly styled a science (as the Lundensians do), or whether it be called a confession, or a churchly activity presupposing faith (Barth), it all amounts to the same thing, so long as Scripture is treated not as the authoritative Word from God, but as an object of critical study, which therefore may be questioned and challenged at any and every point!

In its lucid, reflective moods, Liberalism (this includes NeoOrthodoxy) admits that it does not really regard the Bible as the Word of God, and that this is the decisive difference, the unbridgeable gulf between itself and Orthodoxy:

. . . the base question, the theological Great Divide, is still the question about the Word of God and the words of the Bible. How is the Word of God related to the Bible? Is the Bible the Word or is the Word in the Bible? Every agreement elsewhere in theological discussion means nothing unless the approaches to consensus have begun on the same side of this divide. No development yet in sight suggests any will or way to tunnel through, either. The much discussed conservatizing of liberals and liberalizing of conservatives is fun to think about, but on the only point worth discussing discussion is beside the point. There are clear alternatives that can be defended, but these are prior, continuing and ultimate alternatives which only sloppy analysis or doomed expectation could ever suggest were elidable. What real difference does it make whether right moves left and left moves right if, when they get to easier hailing distance, the gulf or ridge between is impassable, if there is no footing in the middle, if a clear and decisive choice still has to be made?

Today, Protestant theology everywhere outside the self-consciously conservative wing has chosen for the side which says with Fosdick that the Bible "*contains* the word of God but not that it *is* the word of God" ... The discussion that continues on this latter side may have by-passed Fosdick's specific suggestions and terms, just as it may someday re-incorporate some of them, only to criticise them once more. But that discussion is all on Fosdick's side of the divide.[47]

On the issue of the relation of the Word of God to the Scriptures, then,

Neo-Orthodoxy occupies the same ground as the older form of Liberalism. Unfortunately, however, traditional theological terms are often used so loosely and unscrupulously, that the mere assertion that "the Bible is the Word of God", by itself, means little or nothing nowadays.

Scripture is really regarded as God's Word only when it is accepted as *in toto* divinely inspired. And "inspiration" here means not anything vague, like a mere influence, or worse, a mere inference from topics or effects ("it is inspired because it treats of Christ"), but something very specific, namely a genuine form of revelation. To assert, therefore, that Scripture is not revelation, but a mere "witness" to revelation, as Modern Theology keeps repeating with an annoying, because totally unwarranted, air of originality and novelty, is to deny that Scripture is in any real sense the inspired Word of God. A divine *word* which however is not a divine *revelation,* is an absurd and impossible notion, and certainly an unscriptural one. It is clear, then, that Verbal Inspiration, in the Church's traditional, plenary sense, is the only Christian doctrine, or inspiration, "verbal" referring not to the "how" but to the "what", i.e., the words *(verba),* of which "all Scripture" (the explicit object of inspiration, II Tim. 3: 16) consists. And at one time the term "Verbal Inspiration" indeed divided those who believed that Scripture is the Word of God from those who did not. Today, however, even "Verbal Inspiration", by itself, means very little. Modern-Theology has devised the curious theory, not to say sophistry, that all the words of Scripture can be "inspired" (this means merely that they somehow "bear witness" to Christ), while at the same time they are, in the words of a previous quote, "thoroughly human and fallible"! John Baillie, for example, has written:

> Here, then, we have the main respect in which the teaching alike of Romanism and of what Dr. Barth calls "the later Old Protestantism" (here the fable of a conflict between Luther and Orthodoxy is trotted out again!-K.M.) is challenged by more recent Protestant theology. What is denied is the *inerrancy of Scripture,* which is the same as to say its *plenary inspiration.* Sometimes the phrase to be tossed back and forth between the controversialists has been "literal inspiration", but this is an ambiguous phrase and has led to confusion. More commonly the change of outlook has been spoken of as a denial of "verbal inspiration", but this is even more misleading. For on the one hand it is not only in respect of their choice of words to express their thoughts and affirmations that we are unable to claim inerrancy for the Biblical writers, but in respect of their thoughts and affirmations themselves. Nothing could be more artificial than to suppose that these writers were endowed with infallibility in all that they had in mind to say, while the Holy Spirit left them to their own devices as to how they should say it. Hence, on the other hand we should have no hesitation in affirming that inspiration extended not only to the thought of the writers, but to the very words they employed in the expression of these thoughts; though in neither case can we say that the inspiration was plenary. If then the inspiration is not regarded as plenary, there is no reason why we should not be-

lieve in verbal inspiration.[48]

What an excruciating torture of language and logic!

Now, the Formal Principle of Sacred Theology means, basically, letting God's Word be God's Word in theory and in practice. And just as obedience to the Lordship of Christ entails more than a mere babbling of "Lord, Lord", so obedience to His Word entails vastly more than mere ritual incantations employing phrases like "Word of God", "inspiration", etc. Whether men *call* the Bible the "Word of God" is not yet decisive; whether they *treat* it as such, is!

The Bible is not treated, *bona fide,* as the inspired Word of God, unless it is also accepted as inerrant. To say that the original autographs of the Sacred Scriptures asserted (not merely reported! For example, words and acts of Satan, Judas, etc., are correctly reported, but they are not approved or asserted), or at least might have asserted, incorrect, erroneous notions, is to deny that Scripture is really the Word of God, even though that title may, *honoris causa,* be bestowed upon Scripture! To be the Word of God and to contain even the possibility of error, are two totally incompatible qualities. The concept of an "erring Word of God", no matter how carefully hidden in pietistic verbal fog, is a monstrous self-contradiction from the point of view of natural reason alone, and is nothing short of blasphemy from the point of view of faith. *Inerrancy* is thus a reliable indicator of whether the statement: "Scripture is the Word of God" means anything real, or whether it is simply an instance of a loose use of language. Dr. C. F. W. Walther, who exposed relentlessly the cant of the "conservative" or "Positive" theology of his day, wrote:

> It is absolutely necessary that we maintain the doctrine of inspiration as taught by our orthodox dogmaticians. If the possibility that Scripture contained the least error were admitted, it would become the business of *man* to sift the truth from the error. That places man *over Scripture,* and Scripture is *no longer* the source and norm of doctrine. Human reason is made the *norma* of truth, and Scripture is degraded to the position of a *norma normata.* The least deviation from the old inspiration doctrine introduces a rationalistic germ into theology and infects the whole body of doctrine.[49]

Dr. F. Bente, who also had the gift of "discerning the spirits" keenly and penetratingly, wrote:

> It may at first sight look like an unwarranted statement, but it is actually so: the denial of the doctrine of inspiration overthrows the Christian theology. The Christian doctrines may indeed still stand for a time; but the entire theological edifice is undermined and hollowed out if it is no longer borne by the inspired, infallible word of Scripture . . . If theology gives up the inspiration of Scripture, if the Bible is no longer the infallible Word of God but a human, fallible record of the things of which it treats, the *loci classici* and *dicta probantia* are no longer of any avail. A veritable deluge of all manner of skeptical questions concerning the origin and content of Scripture is unloosed which cannot be checked and controlled.[50]

When, during doctrinal discussions in 1939, the official commissioners of the United Lutheran Church in America claimed that they accepted

52

the doctrine of inspiration of Scripture, but declared themselves "unable to accept the statement of the Missouri Synod that the Scriptures are the infallible truth 'also in those parts which treat of historical, geographical, and other secular matters, John 10:35,'" Dr. T. Engelder pointed out, quite justly, that the distinction between the Scriptural *doctrine* or fact of inspiration on the one hand, and an allegedly narrower, man-made *"theory"* of *Verbal* Inspiration and Inerrancy, on the other, was "a clumsy form of sophistry. It deals with an 'inspiration' which is not real inspiration."[51]

Contemporary discussion forces upon us a consideration of two questions:

(1) What are the grounds for the Church's belief in the Inerrancy of Scripture?

(2) What is the meaning of that belief?

As for the first question, one often encounters the notion that insistence on the Inerrancy is not at all "Biblical", that it is in fact a piece of "philosophy", and that in any case it is some sort of new, weird, sectarian exaggeration, which is found neither in the Symbolical Books of the Lutheran Church, nor in the writings of the great Reformer, but arose mainly out of the Fundamentalist Modernist controversy of this century! What are the facts of the case?

Aside from the many passages in the Confessions, which identify Scripture with the Word of God, and attribute individual Biblical words to the. Holy Ghost, there is the rather explicit statement in the *Large Catechism,* IV *(de baptismo),* 57: "The Word of God can neither err nor deceive *(nec potest errare nec fallere)"*. Inerrancy and Infallibility (note the identical roots!) mean exactly that, no more and no less. Informed liberals admit that "a literally infallible Bible . . . verbally inspired" is "an assumption implied throughout the Lutheran Symbols."[52]

As for the claim that Luther took a more "liberal" view of Scripture than did Lutheran Orthodoxy, Dr. F. Pieper devotes a whole chapter in his *Dogmatics* to its refutation. He concludes:

It is thus evident that the modern theologians who claim Luther as patron of their liberal attitude toward Scripture either have not read Luther at all, but have copied from compilations of others without verifying them, or, if they have actually read Luther, were unable to understand him, because their wish to have Luther as their protector was stronger than their sense of historical truth.[53]

In 1944 Dr. Michael Reu published his celebrated book *Luther and the Scriptures,* which supports the same conclusion. The most painstaking treatment of which we are aware, from a translation of a review in the *Svensk Pastoraltidsskrift* of September 1, 1960, is a 499 page treatise by E. Thestrup Pedersen.[54] This book is a dispassionate, scholarly analysis not of what his modern interpreters *claim* Luther said, but of what he actually did say and write. Pedersen shows that the "liberal" interpretation of Luther, so popular in Sweden, is a complete falsification of the historical Luther.

We come now to Scripture's own claims about itself. At this point a very basic misunderstanding must be removed. The extraordinary notion appears to have gained currency, that to consult the Scriptures on the subject of Inerrancy, means something like this: First one looks through the Scriptures, with special attention to the alleged errors and contradictions, pointed out by the critics. Next, one decides that there must be something to these allegations, since "where there is smoke there is fire". Finally, one concludes either that the "Biblical evidence" does not support the claim of Inerrancy, or else that the definition of Inerrancy must be stretched to accommodate also its opposite, i.e., the possibility of errors, or, more politely, "discrepancies", which the "Biblical evidence," supposedly suggests. This new, allegedly "Biblical" definition of Inerrancy thus turns out to be a contradiction in terms, i.e., an "inerrancy" which also allows for "errors", an obvious absurdity probably tolerated only in "theology"! The trouble with this whole procedure is that it does not even remotely begin to do what it claims to be doing, i.e., to determine the Scriptural position on Inerrancy!

Inerrancy, like every other Christian doctrine, rests on clear texts of Scripture, in other words on divine authority, accepted by faith, not on any sort of human experimentation and *a posteriori* judgment, which is exactly what the above procedure is. To examine the Scripture, with a view of determining empirically, from one's own research, whether or not it is in fact inerrant, is like trying to test the doctrine of the Real Presence by examining a wafer under a microscope! Just as the doctrine of the Real Presence rests on the clear Scripture texts which teach it, not on any human investigations, so the doctrine of the Inerrancy rests on those clear Scripture texts which teach it, and not on a human examination of "the evidence". In other words, we are certain of the Inerrancy *a priori,* on the grounds of self-authenticating divine authority, not *a posteriori* on the grounds of our own empirical observations and conclusions. The former position is Christian Theology, the latter is the critical, "scientific" method of subjectivism and skepticism.

It should be clear, on the basis of the preceding, that since the doctrine of Inspiration and Inerrancy does not rest upon a human examination of the inspired text, the availability or unavailability of the original autographs in no way affects the doctrine. We note in passing that it was of the current *copies* of Scripture that Christ said: "They *have* Moses and the Prophets" (St. Luke 16: 29), and that He guaranteed the presence of His undistorted Word to His Church in perpetuity, St. Matt. 28: 20, St. John 8: 31-32, St. John 17: 20. "Likewise in His temptation (Matthew 4) Christ operates with the *gegraptai* as with an immovable certain text. We do not read that the devil brought up the matter of 'variant readings,'"[55] none of which, incidentally, in any way threatens a single doctrine of the Christian religion. We conclude with Dr. Pieper therefore:

> So we know *a priori,* before any investigation, from the promise and the testimony of Christ, that in the Scriptures now at the disposal of the Church we have a reliable text, or in other words, the authentic doctrine of the Apostles and Prophets, that is, of God, in spite of the *variae lectiones* in the copies.[56]

54

What then does Scripture itself teach concerning its Inerrancy? Scripture teaches its own Inerrancy wherever it teaches that it is the inspired Word of God, the "oracles of God" *(logia tou theou,* Rom. 3: 2). Even Aulen appears to admit that Inerrancy is a necessary consequence of a real Inspiration: "If every syllable in the Bible is inspired (this is exactly what 2 Tim. 3: 16 teaches! K.M.), all statements have the same binding authority, since there can be no different degrees of divine authority."[57] Since God is omniscient, and does not lie, His Word is truth (St. John 17: 17), and this not in any vague or general sense, but categorically, in reality. And in an earlier section we have disposed of the modern sophistry according to which "truth" in the Bible does not mean correctness (a quality of propositions), but merely some sort of loyalty or faithfulness (a quality of persons). Dr. Pieper's perspective is quite Biblical when he says:

> A Bible in which the boundaries between divine truth and human error would forever be uncertain would indeed be a fitting controversial subject for theologians of the school of Lessing, but would certainly not be the Book of which David says: "The testimony of the Lord is sure, making wise the simple" (Ps. 19 : 17), and: "Thy Word is a lamp unto my feet and a light unto my path" (Ps. 119: 105).[58]

Furthermore, it is easy to show that Christ and His Holy Apostles, whose example is normative for the Church, accepted the Old Testament as absolutely authoritative and infallible. St. John 10: 35: "Scripture cannot be broken", is a parenthesis introduced by Our Lord as self-evident and axiomatic. He applies it, moreover, not to some Messianic or Christological "quintessence" of the Gospel, but to a rather peripheral, apparently insignificant little quote from the Psalter! This little text "cannot be broken" not because of any obviously stupendous value inherent in it, but simply because it is part of "the Scripture"! Nor does Christ permit any appeal from an "inferior" Scripture to the Lord of Scripture: "If you believed Moses, you would believe Me, for he wrote of Me. But if you do not believe his writing, how will you believe My words?" (St. John 5: 46-47). And Christ's Apostle declares: "so worship I the God of my fathers, believing *all things* which are written in the law and in the prophets" (Acts 24: 14). The Christian reason for believing anything is the fact that it is written in the authoritative Scripture, not one's own speculations and preferences-a *la smorgasbord*—*as* to the merits of the contents!

And what is true of the Old Testament, is also true of the Word of Christ, whether spoken directly by Him, or indirectly, through His inspired Evangelists and Apostles: "Whosoever therefore shall be ashamed of Me and of My words in this adulterous and sinful generation; of him also shall the Son of man be ashamed, when he cometh in the glory of His Father with the holy angels" (St. Mark 8:38); "He that heareth you heareth Me; and he that despiseth you despiseth Me" (St. Luke IO: 16); "If I have told you earthly things, and ye believe not, how shall ye believe, if I tell you of heavenly things?" (St. John 3: 12); "If they have kept My saying, they will keep yours also" (St. John 15: 20); "We speak, not in the words which man's wisdom teacheth, but which the Holy Ghost teacheth" (I Cor. 2: 13); "And are built upon the foundation of the apostles and prophets, Jesus Christ Himself being the Chief Corner Stone" (Eph. 2: 20).

Recently the writer attended a lecture, in Brisbane, by a sectarian seminary-professor, who, it appeared, was much enamored of the latest British "Biblical Theology". The professor began by showing, on the basis of the New Testament, that for Christ and His Apostles the Old Testament was indeed the infallible, absolutely authoritative Word of God, which could not be questioned or criticized at any point. The lecturer quite capably refuted a number of sophistries which have been invented to explain away the New Testament data, and showed that no other conclusion, with respect to the absolute authority of the Old Testament for Christ and His Apostles, comported with honest and competent scholarship. Having thus stated and documented the position of Christ and His Apostles, the professor continued nonchalantly: "The question is whether we are bound to follow their example"! This he then proceeded vigorously to claim, on the grounds of the kenotic theory that Jesus, and naturally also His disciples, were children of their times, and subject to the prejudices and errors of their day!

Such an attitude is unthinkable for the Christian Church. The mere question, not to mention the negative response, whether we are bound to the "views" of Christ and the Apostles, amounts to a "stepping out of one's Baptism", to use a memorable phrase coined by Dr. M. Franzmann. To question the teaching authority of Christ's Apostles is an attack upon, and a negation of the apostolicity of the Church, and a rebellion against the Lord Who invested His Apostles with teaching authority. But to question directly the teaching authority of Christ Himself is open disavowal of, and contempt for that "Lordship of Christ", of which the moderns like to talk so much. Christian Theology, bound as she is to her Lord's Scripture, is not authorized even to treat such sacrilege as debatable within her domains! And it must surely be clear that if Christ and His Apostles did not possess, in their pristine purity, the real teachings of the Christian religion, then no such teachings exist; for if they were not available to the divine Founder of the Church, then certainly no sensible person two thousand years later can hope to discover them!

Dr. Martin Franzmann, in his essay "The Posture of the Interpreter",[59] shows that the Christian theologian is bound to a *mimesis* ("imitation", cf. 1 Cor. 4: 16 *et al.)* of the Apostles. With panoramic, one is tempted to say "prophetic", vision, Dr. Franzmann surveys the field and asks: "If modern Old Testament exegesis ... has made dubious and problematical what is for the apostles certain and axiomatic ... if modern methodology in Old Testament exegesis has brought men to the point where they can no longer 'imitate' the apostles, may it not be that we are in the last stages of a grandiose aberration, comparable to the age-long domination of the four-fold sense in patristic and medieval exegesis?" The cure is not of course to be expected from quarters which are committed to the very soul and source of the "grandiose aberration:" the denial of the Formal

56

Principle of Sacred Theology, i.e., the absolute authority of Holy Writ!

What must be clearly seen, therefore, is that to deny or question, in deference to Modern Theology, the Inerrancy of Scripture, is not merely a question of a "new approach", or a "different theological method", etc., which must be given its trial, but it is in fact a bold disavowal and repudiation not merely of apostolicity, but of the authority of Christ Himself, in short, it is heresy, apostasy of the most serious and destructive sort, no matter how thickly it be sugarcoated with protestations of reverence for the "Lordship of Christ"! The choice is not between two different "versions" or "alternatives" *within* Christian Theology, but between Christian Theology and an extraneous, paganizing imitation. If men wish to found a new religion, then, in our "enlightened", pluralistic age they have the legal right to do so. But if they admittedly teach something different than what Christ taught, and substitute their own authority for the authority of Christ, why must they call their religion Christianity?

Having examined the grounds of the Church's belief in the Inerrancy of Scripture, we turn now to our second question: What is the meaning of that belief?

To call a piece of gold-plated lead a bar of gold, does not make it such, although the claim may succeed in trapping an unsuspecting purchaser. Similarly, the mere fact that one uses the term "inerrancy" does not, unfortunately, mean that one is using that word in its only rightful, proper sense. Inerrancy, for example, is not the same as "reliability", which is a far more general, much vaguer concept. Inerrancy means a total absence of formal error. And not merely the fact of error, but even its possibility, must be denied *a priori,* if Scripture is truly regarded as the Word of God.

To say that the Inerrancy of Scripture means merely that it says what God wishes it to say and that it conveys divine power which engenders and sustains faith in Christ, is really a total denial of Inerrancy. It is a form of pragmatism: Something is true because it "works", or has this or that beneficial effect! Either "inerrancy" means what it says, i.e., absence of error, or it does not, but then some other words should be used. No matter how much pietistic prattling is added to confuse the issue, "inerrancy" can never mean: "the ability to perform a certain function, despite the presence of factual errors and contradictions". Why should one say "inerrancy" when one means the opposite? To say that Scripture is inerrant because it leads to salvation, is no less absurd than to say: "Spiders are beautiful because they catch insects", or: "Camels are inerrant because they carry heavy loads to their proper destinations, and do not require water very often".

Futhermore, Scripture is either inerrant in all matters of which it treats, or it is not inerrant at all. To distinguish here between "religious, theological" statements or "matters of salvation" on the one hand, and information on "secular subjects" on the other, and then to exempt the latter from Inerrancy, is totally illicit. Every statement of Scripture, even if it should touch on "secular subjects," is *ipso facto* religious and theological. The above distinction is, moreover, totally unworkable, for what is "essential" or "theological" to one, may not be to another. For Bultmann, even the Resurrection of Christ is a mere symbol, and for Tillich even the existence of a a personal God is not a part of the Bible's "essential" or "theological" message! Barth, as we have seen, is quite consistent in denying the Inerrancy of Scripture also in matters of religion or theology.

Aulen also sees the issue quite clearly:

> If the validation cannot be based on the theory of verbal inspiration, neither is it possible to select certain portions of the Bible as infallible authority. Even such an abbreviated Biblicism is impossible in whatever form it appears: whether certain definite books or certain portions are accepted, or an appeal is made to "the teaching of Jesus". The attempt to determine beforehand by means of certain mechanical rules what passages are infallibly inspired leads to arbitrariness and absurdity.[60]

Despite this and other crass denials of Scriptural authority, not to mention Inerrancy, Aulen, incidentally, has devised for himself a special sense, in which he finds it possible to assert that "the evangelical principle of Scripture as the 'only infallible rule of faith and life' is forever valid"!

Heresy has a way of hollowing out traditional, orthodox terms (this is called "theological discussion"), and then, when their substance no longer stands in the way, rushing past and engulfing them, leaving their empty facades more or less intact, but desolate, isolated in a sea of alien and hostile currents. This happens to Inerrancy when the term is allowed to stand, as a sort of phantom land-mark for naive travelers, while its substance is in practice totally ignored. And the practice in question is the so-called Higher Criticism, that is, the application of the "historical-critical" method to the Scriptures. The "historical-critical" method is simply the general Scientific Method, as applied to the study of ancient historical documents. In other words, in seeking to determine the origin and meaning of the various parts of the Bible, the historical-critical method must in principle treat the Bible like Shakespeare's plays, Aesop's Fables, or any other literary work of the past. The method cannot possibly, without committing suicide, employ such "unscientific" considerations as divine authority or inspiration in arriving at its conclusions.

If the issue were always stated in such bald terms, so that it would be quite clear that it is a question of substituting Scientific Method, in short, *human* authority and ingenuity, for faith in *divine* authority, the apostasy would be rather obvious and could be advocated only *extra ecclesiam* ...Those who seek to make the validity of the historical-critical method plausible in conservative circles, however, disarm much of the opposition by protesting complete allegiance to the divine authority of Scripture. They argue that Scripture has a "divine side", to be accepted by faith, and a "human side", to be investigated by means of strictly historical research. Putting it differently, on the "faith-side" all of Scripture is to be accepted as authoritative, while on its "history side" the Scientific Method is to be allowed free reign.

The "faith-side" can only be accepted on faith, or rejected, and no proof in either direction is possible. The "history side", however, has taken place in a human context, and hence as history must be measurable and expressible in terms of ordinary human experience, using all the normal tools of historiography, psychology, sociology, etc. This will be as true of the "history side" of God's revelation as of any natural historical process in which there is no "faith side" or revelation . . . In other words, we must do justice to the human (historical) side of Scripture as well as to the divine side (without using these terms improperly, as some do).[61]

Perhaps this has a ring of plausibility and harmlessness for those not initiated into the deeper mysteries of Modern Theology. The real import of those few sentences becomes much clearer when we ponder what follows, in the same essay:

Christian scholars may often champion the same opinions as agnostics (on the "historical side"), but with totally different presuppositions (on the "faith side").

If Scripture has a historical side ... it follows that historical truths about it are discoverable only by the all-too-human process of trial and error, of experimentation, testing, etc. ... "Historical" exegesis simply attempts to state with utmost candor the meaning of the O.T. text to the believer at the time of its revelation, together with whatever incompleteness, immaturity, and opaqueness it finds there. "Theological" exegesis, on the contrary, recognizes that a final definitive revelation has been given the Church in the N.T., and thus for the Church's use attempts to fill the incomplete with the complete and interpret the unclear by means of the clear (i.e., a specifically Christian motivation will be given the O.T. ethos, the "fulfillment" of much that may have been understood differently at the time it was revealed will be recognized, etc.). Historical exegesis alone must inevitably become judaistic (as Judaism is based on the O.T.) ...

Most current critical opinions on the date and authorship of O.T. books are based on such reasoning- and we can scarcely deny the validity of such a methodology (aside from details of conclusions) without negating all that we have stated earlier in this essay.[62]

It is true, unfortunately, that the more general the principle, the more destructive it really is if false, and the more harmless it appears to the innocent by-stander! Somehow people do not become too upset when it is proposed that "matters of isagogics" should be left to ordinary historical-critical study. After all, "isagogics" (the discipline of Biblical Introduction, dealing with the date and authorship of the various portions of the Bible) seems so peripheral, so far removed from the central truths of the Faith; and besides, the very technical term itself seems to convey the sort of soothing and reassuring effect which patients feel when their doctors with an air of confidence and efficiency, give a Latin name to some dread malady! To have swallowed "toxic fluorides" seems almost delicious, and certainly preferable to a dose of cod-liver oil. To discover that it is rat-poison one has taken is somewhat more distressing! It is also much more distressing if for "isagogics" we substitute some specific, illustrative examples.

In His controversy with the Pharisees, recorded in St. Matthew 22: 41-45, our Lord quotes the 110th Psalm ("The Lord said unto my Lord.."), and attributes the quote to David, in such a way that His whole argument depends upon the Davidic authorship...For Christian Theology the case is settled. If Christ says that David uttered the words in question, then David did, and the subject is no longer debatable. This historical-critical method, however, reasons thus: The authorship of Psalm 110 is a problem in Isagogics, and belongs to the Bible's "history-side". Therefore the question of authorship cannot be settled *a priori,* by an appeal to authority, but must be reserved for "the all-too-human process of trial and error, or experimentation, testing, etc." Now, obviously one cannot apply here the historical-critical method, without first granting that Christ made a mistake, either deliberately, by arguing from premises He knew to be false, or else, inadvertently, out of ignorance!

Going beyond Isagogics, to the matter of a distinction between a "historical" and a "theological" exegesis, let us look at St. John 12:41, which records Our Lord's assertion that Isaiah saw Christ's glory, and spoke of Him. Again, for the Christian Church this settles the matter. From the historical-critical viewpoint, however, one must say: The question of what Isaiah knew and meant, belongs to the domain of historical science, and therefore cannot be determined by a reference to New Testament authority. The original meaning of Isaiah's writings have nothing to do with any direct predictions about a personal Messiah, since that concept arose only at a much later date. St. John 12:41, therefore, is to be accepted not as the real, intended, historical meaning of Isaiah, but only as New Testament "theological interpretation" ("faith-side"!), which gives us a fuller meaning for the book of Isaiah, a meaning, however, which was neither known nor intended by the original writer! The same method is then applied wherever the New Testament interprets the Old. Quite apart from the *hybris* of this approach, it is manifestly absurd: The Jewish audiences to which Christ and His Apostles spoke, would hardly have been impressed by anyone who claimed merely to be reading things into the Old Testament which were not actually there! The whole approach of the New Testament is that these things *are* there, and that if they were not, Christianity would be a fraud. Such happens to be the original historical foundation of the Christian religion. One cannot very well come along at this late date, and supply some new and different foundation, without abandoning the original structure altogether!

It must surely be evident, therefore, how disastrous is the principle that in "isagogical and exegetical questions" no dogmatically binding positions exist, and that the individual is automatically free to adopt whatever views he prefers, including those suggested by the historical-critical method. In the first place, absolutely *any* doctrine could thus be converted overnight into a wide-open "exegetical problem" (the difference between Lutherans and Calvinists on the Real Presence is an "exegetical problem"!). Secondly, those isagogical questions which are clearly settled by the authority of Scripture, *ipso facto* become points of doctrine, which cannot be denied without repudiating the organic foundation of the Faith! No matter how "small" the point itself may seem, if it is supported by the authority of Christ or His inspired Apostles, then not one inch can be yielded without treason to God, His Word, and His Church.

We hasten to admit that of course in those cases in which we have no clear Biblical *dictum,* human ingenuity is quite free to conjecture and guess-when more important things have been attended to. The point at issue is not whether there are open isagogical and exegetical questions, but whether there are closed ones. And of course, what is decisive is whether Scripture itself not merely the opinion of its interpreters, no matter how eminent, learned, orthodox, or traditional-really does render a clear decision in a given case.

It does not require an extraordinary instinct for consistency, to realize that any meaningful doctrine of Scriptural Inerrancy cannot be combined with an approach which blithely sets aside statements of Scripture, even the *ipsissima verba* of Our Lord Himself, on the pretext that these statements are part of the "human side" of Scripture, and therefore subject to correction by man! And, as has often been pointed out by others, the Christological analogy, frequently invoked by the neologists, is solidly on the side of orthodox Christian Theology: If the "human side" of Scripture is to correspond to the human nature of Christ, then the former implies error just as little as the latter implies sin. The human and the divine simply do not exist side by side in Scripture in such a way that one could say: Here the divine begins and the human ends. Rather, *all* of Scripture is thoroughly human (given in human language, dealing with the humblest topics of human life, having all the peculiarities of style, personality, etc., of its authors, and the like), and *all* of it is divine, and therefore inspired, inerrant, authoritative, and inviolable.

Dr. Walther warned already in 1886, in a striking paraphrase of Dr. Luther's well-known words about Zwingli's *alloeosis:*

> Beware, beware, I say, of this "divine-human Scripture"! It is a devil's mask; for at last it manufactures such a Bible after which I certainly would not care to be a Bible Christian, namely, that the Bible should henceforth be no more than any other good book, a book which I would have to read with constant sharp discrimination in order not to be led into error. For if I believe this, that the Bible contains also errors, it is to me no longer a touchstone but itself stands in need of one. In a word, it is unspeakable what the devil seeks by this "divine-human Scripture" . . . May God have mercy upon His poor Christendom, in these last, sad, and dangerous times![63]

It is in the light of the preceding discussion that we must understand the modern talk about "interpretation" and "hermeneutics", which, to orthodox ears, suggests a wholesome pre-occupation with Scripture. Without a detailed acquaintance with the perspectives of Modern Theology, it is easy to fall prey to the fuzzy notion that modern research has discovered so many new facts about the Bible and its background, that new methods of interpretation are needed to do justice to them, and that this is what Modern Theology does. A far more realistic understanding of what the modern "interpretation" is all about, can be got by analyzing what is hinted at by Dr. W. M. Oesch in these incisive words:

> Modernity rarely denies a truth outright or rejects a witness to the truth directly, as such; modern man helps himself by "Opening new perspectives of hermeneutics (exegesis)", i.e., by "diverting".[64]

Yes, the terms "hermeneutics" and "hermeneutical" are used nowadays in a rather grand, sweeping, and thoroughly false sense. All sorts of anti-Scriptural, critical assumptions are being accommodated under the widened roof of "hermeneutics". Actually, hermeneutics is that branch of Theology which treats of the proper principles of Bible interpretation. The only valid sort of hermeneutical question therefore is: What does Scripture say? or: What must I do to let Scripture interpret itself? The modern question, however, is: Shall I accept what Scripture says? or: How much of what Scripture says shall I accept? *These* questions have nothing whatever to do with hermeneutics. They represent, rather, the critical approach. Hermeneutics seeks merely to understand the Word which it accepts; criticism asks whether and to what extent that which is understood must also be accepted. The basic modern problem is not at all a question of being able to *understand* the Bible, but rather one of being willing to *submit* to it; and that has nothing to do with hermeneutics. The difference between hermeneutics and criticism is the difference between affirmation and denial, obedience and disobedience, faith and unbelief, Theology and skepticism. No neutral territory between them exists.

Just how Biblical modern "Biblical Theology" really is, becomes evident in a rather penetrating, in fact, desperate analysis by one of its representatives. In "Cosmology, Ontology, and the Travail of Biblical Language"[65] Langdon B. Gilkey argues, in essence, as follows: The Biblical writers, the Reformation, and Orthodoxy, all understood the Scriptures literally. Liberalism rebelled against the miraculous element in Scripture, and converted objective miraculous events into subjective experiences and "interpretations" of objectively perfectly ordinary happenings. Neo-orthodoxy and the "Biblical Theology" allied with it, rebelled against this subjectivism, and insisted that God's revelation is objective and prior, and that faith does not produce it but merely responds to it. But, as Gilkey shows, "Biblical Theology" really does not get beyond Schleiermacherian subjectivism, or liberalism, since it accepts the modern philosophical world-view, and therefore cannot accept the Scriptural accounts as literal fact and history. When "Biblical Theology" therefore repeats Biblical-sounding phrases, these are really without meaning. Some excerpts from this significant article follow:

> My own confusion results from what I feel to be the basic posture, and problem of contemporary theology: it is half liberal and modern, on the one hand, and half biblical and orthodox, on the other, i.e., its world view or cosmology is modern, while its theological language is biblical and orthodox ...

Thus contemporary theology does not expect, nor does it speak of, wondrous divine events on the surface of natural and historical life ... Now this assumption of a causal order among phenomenal events, and therefore of the authority of the scientific interpretation of observable event, makes a great difference to the validity one assigns to biblical narratives and so to the way one understands their meaning. Suddenly a vast panoply of divine deeds and events recorded in Scripture are no longer regarded as having actually happened ... all these "acts" vanish from the plane of historical reality and enter the, never-never land of "religious interpretation" by the Hebrew people . . . Nor do we believe, incidentally, that God could have done or commanded certain "unethical" deeds like destroying Sodom and Gomorrah or commanding the murder of the Amalekites. The modern assumption of the world order has stripped bare our view of the biblical history of all the divine deeds observable on the surface of history, as our modern humanitarian ethical view has stripped the biblical God of most of his mystery and offensiveness (!). . . For us, then, the Bible is a book of the acts Hebrews believed God might have done and the words he might have said had he done and said them—but of course we recognize he did not. The difference between this view of the Bible as a parable illustrative of Hebrew religious faith and the view of the Bible as a direct narrative of God's actual deeds and words is so vast that it scarcely needs comment. It makes us wonder, despite ourselves, what, in fact, do we moderns think God did in the centuries preceding the incarnation, what *were* his mighty acts? ... Thus while the language of biblical theology is God-centered, the whole is included within gigantic parentheses marked "human religion" ... "Are the main words and categories in biblical theology meaningful?"

. . . If they are in fact being used as analogies (God acts, but not as men act; God speaks, but not with an audible voice), do we have any idea at all to what sort of deed or communication these analogies refer? Or are they just serious sounding, biblical-sounding, and theological-sounding words to which we can, if pressed, assign no meaning? ... Perhaps the most important theological affirmation that modern biblical theology draws from the Scripture is that God is he who acts, meaning by this that God does unique and special actions in history. And yet when we ask: "All right, what has he done?" no answer can apparently be given. Most of the acts recorded in Scripture turn out to be "interpretations by Hebrew faith", and we are sure that they, like the miracles of the Buddha, did not really happen at all. And the one remaining objective act, the Exodus, becomes on analysis "the East wind blowing over the Red Sea" ... If this is what we mean, then clearly we have left the theological framework of "mighty act with faith response" and returned to Schleiermacher's liberalism, in which God's general activity is consistent throughout the continuum of space-time events and in which special religious feeling apprehends the presence of God in and through ordinary finite events ... despite our Bowery theological language, our actual understanding of Hebrew religion remains enclosed within liberal categories ... We say the biblical God acts, but we can give neither concrete examples nor analogical description; we say he speaks, and no illustrative dialogues can be specified. What has happened is that as modern men perusing the Scriptures, we have rejected as invalid all the innumerable cases of God's acting and speaking; but as neo-orthodox men looking for a word from the Bible, we have induced from these cases the theological generalization that God is he who acts and speaks. This general truth about God we then assert while denying all the particular cases on the basis of which the generalization was first made. Consequently, biblical theology is left with a set of theological abstractions, more abstract than the dogmas of scholasticism, for these are concepts with no known concreteness. Finally, our language is self-contradictory because, while we use the language of orthodoxy, what we really mean is concepts and explanations more appropriate to liberal religion. For if there is any middle ground between the observable deed and the audible dialogue which we reject, and what the liberals used to call religious experience and religious insight, then it has not yet been spelled out. [66]

We have quoted so extensively from this rather devastating admission of utter insolvency, both spiritual and intellectual, made on behalf of Modern Theology, in order that it might be quite clear what this "theology" means when it styles itself "interpretation."

The "interpretation" really amounts to a rather thorough-going transmutation: The theological product of the Bible must first be broken down, by means of the historical-critical method. Everything unacceptable to "modern man" is stripped away, like the layers of an onion, and discarded as an outworn "philosophical framework" (clearly but another version of the "human" or "history-side" of Scripture). What one regards as the real core, or "theological significance" the moderns care nothing about any Biblical event, fact, or doctrine, but only about its "theological significance" is then placed into a more modern "philosophical framework", and everyone is immensely pleased at having restated the "old truth" in a "new way" and at having "liberated" Theology from the clutches of "philosophy". Upon moderately close inspection, however, the "liberation" turns out to be liberated Theology from everything except words! What it really comes to, is that any and all definite meanings of Biblical terms and concepts are drained off as "philosophy", and Theology is left holding empty verbal bags, which anyone may fill with whatever content he pleases! This whole process of dismantling and re-assembling is really a sort of theological taxidermy: As a bird must first be killed, opened, and disemboweled, in order then to be stuffed and sewn together again, so all the living content of Scripture must first be removed—as "philosophy" of course!–so that a new, more manageable content may be put in, before the old plumage of Biblical phrases and expressions is sewn together again! The resulting resemblances may be ever so striking, but they re-

64

main-resemblances: As the stuffed bird is no longer a bird, so the denatured "Biblical Theology" is no longer Biblical Theology.

Even when Christian beliefs, or fragments thereof, are present through a felicitous inconsistency-in the final, "dressing-up" stage of the "re-interpretation", they are worked into the finished product not *by* virtue of any methodological necessity, but simply by virtue of the "interpreter's" personal preference. This arbitrary element of personal, subjective taste or whim explains why there exists such a wide range of clashing "interpretations". And "those who get over all these abysses and reconcile all these wars by talking about 'aspects of truth'," have been sufficiently answered by the witty Mr. G. K. Chesterton:

> I will only say here that this seems to me an evasion which has not even had the sense to disguise itself ingeniously in words. If we talk of a certain thing being an aspect of truth, it is evident that we claim to know what is truth; just as, if we talk of the hind leg of a dog, we claim to know what is a dog. Unfortunately, the philosopher who talks about aspects of truth generally also asks, "What is truth?" Frequently even he denies the existence of truth or says it is inconceivable by the human intelligence. How, then, can he recognize its aspects? I should not like to be an artist who brought an architectural sketch to a builder saying, "This is the south aspect of Sea-View Cottage. Sea-View Cottage, of course, does not exist". I should not even like very much to have to explain, under such circumstances, that Sea-View Cottage might exist, but was unthinkable by the human mind. Nor should I like any better to be the bungling and absurd metaphysician who professed to be able to see everywhere the aspects of a truth that is not there.[67]

The crux of the matter is that in modern theological methodology, faith is totally absent from the premises. Its supposed later introduction into the "interpretation" of a product obtained from other sources and by other means, often amounts to little more than the application of a decorative veneer of Christian verbiage! Alien philosophical content is dressed up in "Biblical" language, phrases, "imagery", etc. This disguise appears to be a pietistic attempt to create an illusion of quality (piety, warmth) for an otherwise intolerably cold, quantitative "theological science", which is nothing more than a manipulation of methods, of soulless techniques!

It must be abundantly clear that (1) without Inerrancy the doctrine of Inspiration, and therefore the *sola Scriptura* principle itself, mean nothing and (2) if Inerrancy is to be more than an empty slogan, it must entail some rather rigorous consequences for one's whole approach to Scripture, excluding particularly, *e limine,* the well-nigh universally practiced historical-critical method!

All attempts to isolate within Scripture some sort of "human side," on which "scientific" criticism may safely be practiced, really involve a total repudiation of Scriptural authority. Professed reverence for the "divine side" is mere lip-service, for this "divine side" is not an independent, self-determining entity, which could exercise authority in any practical sense, but it is a mere phantom, hovering precariously in mid-air, without any particular connection to anything specific. Autonomous man, wielding the Scientific Method, is the real authority, which decides what shall be the "human side" and what shall be the "divine side". The latter is merely tolerated temporarily, as a sort of *terra incognita,* in which uncivilized religious imagination may roam freely until such a time as Science may see fit to push its frontiers further. Since "theology" is thus merely a captive province of Science, no conflict between the two is possible: "theology" simply abdicates in advance, on behalf of the Bible of course, in favour of the Scientific Method, at every possible point of conflict! This, incidentally, accounts for the pseudointellectual appeal and respectability of Neo-Orthodoxy, whose split level, schizophrenic footing in both Scriptural authority *and* human science thus turns out to mean a total surrender to the latter! Neo-Orthodoxy, or rather, Neo-Liberalism, repudiates the Formal Principle of Sacred Theology. Its real authority is carnal, worldly wisdom, whose god is the Scientific Method!

Actually, the moderns might and should have learned at least from Kierkegaard, if Scripture alone is not regarded as sufficient, that the strictly objective, descriptive, "scientific" stance-valuable though it be in its proper field, *i.e.,* when investigating such matters of minor import as sulfuric acid or nuclear fission- is pure illusion in the area of Theology. The unregenerate, carnal, natural mind is enmity against God, Rom. 8: 7; I Cor. 2:14. The regenerate mind, on the other hand, subjects itself entirely to the divine authority of Scripture, II Cor. 10:5; St. Luke 10:16; Acts 24:14. Between these two states no neutral ground, no third alternative exists! "He that is not with Me is against Me," St. Mathew 12:30.

Theology, Dogma, and Certainty

Historic Christian Theology and the neo-liberal activity known as "theology" in fashionable, "enlightened" ecclesiastical circles throughout the world, really have little more than the name in common. The two definitions of "theology" are worlds apart. For the orthodox Church, much maligned nowadays for her alleged "intellectualism", Theology is first of all the Spirit-given aptitude to apply Law and Gospel to human souls for their salvation. Fashionable "theology" wants to be nothing of the kind- quite apart even from the fact that it is currently not the fashion to believe in such "Greek" concepts as souls anyway, in deference to scientific superstitions which were modern sixty years ago! Today's "theology" stands not for the *application* of truth-Barth somewhere scorns as "blessed possessors" those who believe in a real, available truth but for an eternal *quest* or *search* for truth, under the aegis of the Scientific Method. For an orthodox theologian, truth is the *terminus a quo,* the starting point, the indispensable prerequisite. For the moderns, on the other hand, truth is the *terminus ad quem,* the pot of gold at the end of the rainbow, the ever-receding horizon, which can never be reached, except in infinity-if there be an infinity!

"The object of research is an ideal goal toward which theology can only strive in its endeavor to attain to the truth", [68] writes Swedish "Lutheran" theologian Gustaf Aulen, whose "Lundensian" school is particularly insistent upon the purely "scientific", descriptive, phenomenological nature of theology.

One feels rather like the little boy in the story about the Emperor's new clothes, in calling attention to the obvious but universally ignored fact that Christ founded not a discussion club or a debating society, for the *discovery* of truth, but a teaching Church, for the *proclamation* of it!

Of Modern Theology one could in fact say quite fairly that it is really a program for avoiding truth, not one for finding it. The theory that truth must always be sought means, in practice, that it dare never be found! Any claim to final, absolute truth would obviously amount to an intolerable blasphemy against the Scientific Method. And Modern Theology can do without many things, but the Scientific Method is not one of them. If truth were ever found, then the search for it, i.e., "theology", would have to cease. And so the treadmill grinds on! "The one milks the billy-goat, and the other holds the sieve", as Luther puts it so aptly.

Totally absent from Modern Theology is the concept of *dogma,* doctrine, divinely revealed truth, *doctrina divina.* Orthodox Theology cannot begin its work without dogma; Modern Theology cannot begin until dogma has been abolished. The basic modern dogma is that there is no dogma. Having rejected the Formal Principle, Modern Theology really has no choice but to get rid of the very idea of revealed doctrine by any possible or impossible means. One might note in passing that all the neologists' contrived appeals to "Biblical thought-forms" on this point, are nothing more than attempts to make a virtue out of a rather nasty necessity!

Truth, to the moderns, has become a Platonic dream, some ectoplasmic, tantalizing something, forever floating above, beyond, and behind any and all concrete, particular beliefs, teachings, concepts, creeds, etc. Nothing is absolute except Relativity. There is no certainty except uncertainty. Words like "doctrine" may indeed be used by the practitioners of the modern theological method, but such terms then stand not for any divinely given teaching to be *confessed,* but for more or less inadequate symbols, formulations, "interpretations", etc., which require not *confession,* but *discussion:*

> No one theology or system of doctrine must be identified with the Christian religion . . . Doctrine is not the Gospel, but only an attempt to explain the significance of the Gospel ... doctrines must be re-formulated for every generation ... no particular system of doctrine can ever be final . . . We cannot understand the development of Christian doctrine unless we have a clear grasp of the facts which that doctrine was invented to explain.[69]

"Doctrine" here clearly means something like "theory" or "hypothesis." And sensible people do not *confess* theories, but *discuss* them! "Confession", in modern theological parlance, does not deal with the particular statements of theology, but with some sort of transcendent religious loyalties, which are quite safely outside the arena where conflicting Confessions used to clash in controversy, and where Theological Discussion nowadays stages friendly war games! The particular verbal and conceptual shapes and forms which are the subject matter of "theological science", can only be harmed by Confession, in the old sense; for Confession would mean a sort of spiritual arrested development, a refusal to progress toward "truth". Discussion, on the other hand, is seen as the refining furnace which keeps on improving and purifying that ever churning mass of "insights", "re-interpretations", and the like, which comprises the raw-materials. And some sections of the furnace are more efficient than others. Thus Bultmann, for instance, has succeeded in developing a theological product so refined already, as to be quite ethereal when compared with that rather early solidity and substance (cf. Mk. 14: 9) which has always distinguished the religion of the Incarnation from idealistic religio-philosophical (usually Platonic) alternatives and/or imitations. Tillich too has succeeded in refining Christianity practically to the point of vacuum. Others, usually less consistent thinkers, emulate Nature in abhorring a vacuum, but find themselves unable to repudiate the universally accepted methodology, which inevitably and inexorably dismembers, dissolves, disintegrates, and evaporates all solid positions.

Writing on "The Heart of Confessionalism", Dr. H. Hamann, Sr., also goes to the heart of the modern predicament:

> On the other hand, we must expect to find, and we assuredly do find, great unwillingness on the part of men to commit themselves to any precise and clear-cut doctrinal statement and to confess such doctrines as divine truth, where the position over against the Holy Scriptures is radically wrong or is vitiated in various ways. Such is the case where the Scriptures are indeed formally recognized as the Word of God, but are actually treated as an essentially human book. Such is the case where the attitude toward the Bible is openly rationalistic ... We have the same situation when the Inspiration of the Scriptures is limited so as to make necessary or at least possible the presence of human errors alongside of divine truth. Nor is the situation very different when the denial of the basic clarity or perspicuity of the Scriptures leads to skepticism and uncertainty as to their true sense or meaning; or when men assert that all doctrines, as established by the exegetical process, are largely a matter of "interpretation," so that contrary and contradictory "interpretations" are equally valid; or when men hold that doctrines may be "restated", no matter how wide the gulf that yawns between the original statement and the "restatement", so as to make them acceptable to modern man. Such views of the Scripture cannot possibly result in doctrinal clarity or doctrinal assurance. They usually result in a condition that may be described as *"panta rhei"*—all is in a state of doctrinal flux—and hence in unwillingness or incapability to make firm, assured, definite doctrinal confessions. Confessions that are made from such pre-suppositions are usually of the vaguest and most general kind and are, besides, very flexible because they are open to personal, individual "interpretation".[70]

Orthodox Lutherans may be tempted to think that this process of dissolution poses no threat to themselves, since they are securely and permanently entrenched in Scriptural Orthodoxy, and are thus safely isolated from the fashionable theological devastation. That would be a fatal mistake. Nothing destroys Theology more effectively than just this sort of carnal security. The fact of the matter is that no one who still carries the Old Adam about with him is immune to this potent virus, which exploits every weakness to gain entrance, breaks down resistance, multiplies with startling rapidity, and then spreads the epidemic!

Liberalism has many faces. And to prospective converts from Orthodoxy it naturally does not show the one which says: "There is no truth". In fact, it is doubtful whether many liberals themselves ever dare to gaze directly upon that Medusa! The initial appeal to orthodox enquirers could be quite gentle. At first only an attitude may be implanted. Perhaps the "patient" is trained to become impatient with "scholastic" dogma. Constant repetition conditions him to believe that doctrine, or dogma, is dry, brittle, dead, man-made, while "Biblical Theology" (the respectable, "scientific" kind, of course) is alive, colorful, exciting "three-dimensional", etc. And so there develops a pseudo-Biblicism, which in the name of "Exegesis" creates a prevailing climate of opinion or prejudice against dogma, and of course Dogmatics. The preposterous impression then begins to gain ground that Theology is essentially Exegesis, Bible Interpretation, or rather, in practice, a continuous discussion of exegetical details, while Dogmatics is the study of what narrow-minded scholastics of the past, "the dogmaticians", have said and written! Naturally, in that view Dogmatics becomes a precarious appendage to Church History, barely allowed to exist by a jealous and arrogant pseudo-Exegesis. The latter is easily abetted by a myopic, pietistic "practical" bent, which suggests Chesterton's quip to the effect that no one is more impractical in practice than he who is "practical" in theory! That orthodox circles are not immune to anti-dogmatic bias, is quite evident. Let this sample suffice:

> Does that mean that we are to discard doctrinal sermons and discussions that youth may be served better? That depends on what is meant by teaching doctrine. If it means throwing chunks of abstract doctrine at him in such a way that it remains an irrelevant idea, then the answer is obviously, yes. But this is not teaching doctrine. *This is dogmatics and dogma* and is not the way God has revealed Himself.[71] (our emphasis)

What shall we say then to the modern superstition which regards the dogmatician as a dangerous purveyor of mere traditionalism, a smuggler of human opinion under the flag of divine authority, and which therefore looks to the exegete for instruction in the "Biblical" point of view?

Let the words of Francis Pieper, like a breath of fresh air, dispel the fog:

> Theology is commonly divided into dogmatic, historical, exegetical, and practical theology. And it is the dogma, that is, doctrine of Scripture, which stamps these various branches of theology as theological disciplines and unifies them. It is the function of historical theology not only to give a historically true picture of the events, but also to evaluate these established facts in the light of Scripture.

Historical theology is the divinely taught art of ascertaining from Scripture God's verdict on the historical events and conditions. That is what makes church history a theological discipline. When the church historian judges events according to his subjective view or any other extra-Biblical norm, church history is no longer a theological discipline. A Christian church history shows, says Luther, "how the dear Gospel fared in the world" . . . From the foregoing it is evident that the dogma is the unifying core of the various theological disciplines. The dogma, the Scriptural doctrine, is the essential element in every discipline, which integrates all branches of sacred theology. The dogmatician must also be an exegete, historian, and practical theologian; and likewise the exegete, the historian, and the practical theologian must also be a good dogmatician. Each must be well acquainted with the Scripture doctrine in all its parts. In spite of the demand for an "undogmatic" Christianity, we declare: "Only dogmatics is edifying," namely, dogmatics as *doctrina divina* revealed in Scripture, the only doctrine, which may be taught in Christ's Church. In the Christian Church, doctrine is the all-important thing. The general orders issued by Christ (Matt., 28) read: 'Teaching them to observe all things whatsoever I have commanded you." Let no minister of Jesus Christ, be he theological professor or pastor of a church, forget this. The theologian who no longer believes that "supernatural truths" are imparted through Scripture, through the doctrine of Scripture, but denounces that as conducive to "intellectualism", has lost sight of the obligations of his sacred office. And the pastors, yes, they especially, dare never forget that their paramount business is to preach doctrine, the divine doctrine of Holy Scripture.[72]

Properly understood, then, Exegesis is essentially method, while Dogmatics is essentially content. The two disciplines do not represent different, conflicting positions, i.e., the "Biblical" and the "dogmatical." That would be absurd. Since correct Scriptural content cannot be separated from correct. Scriptural methods of interpretation, it follows that the dogmatician and the exegete are not two different personages, as we are accustomed to assume, nowadays, from the fact of specialization, but are one and the same person. A person who teaches human, unscriptural views in Theology is not merely a poor exegete, but is first of all a poor dogmatician. Since Dogmatics, properly understood, is the presentation of pure, Scriptural truth, a poor dogmatician must be corrected by a better dogmatician, not merely by an exegete! The exegete cannot, in fact, correct the dogmatician, as such, without to that extent becoming a dogmatician himself; and there is no reason to suppose that the dogmatic positions of professional exegetes are inherently more valid than the dogmatic positions of professional dogmaticians. What must be exploded is the whole curious notion that Dogmatics represents mere human tradition and must therefore be placed under the "control" and "correction" of Exegesis, the latter understood not as method, which is also employed by dogmaticians, but institutionally, as so many professors and departments specializing in a field called "Exegesis"! Christ commanded His Church to teach—that means Dogmatics!—not to compile word-studies (quite helpful in their place) or to play with "imagery", "pictures", and "symbols", as institutionalized "Exegesis" does almost exclusively!

What is being controverted here is not of course Exegesis, but the modern caricature of it, which is based, ultimately, upon the assumption that nothing beyond human "interpretations", nothing like divine truth itself, *doctrina divina,* is available to us, and which therefore cannot understand Dogmatics as anything but arrogant traditionalism.

"Bretschneider must admit," wrote Dr. C. F. W. Walther, "that Dogmatics and Christian or Biblical Theology were indeed regarded as *'quite identical'* in our Church, after the Reformation".[73]

Lutherans today must either re-affirm the proposition that Theology, in the objective sense, IS Dogmatics, i.e., *doctrina divina,* or else capitulate unconditionally before modern subjectivism and relativism. No real, permanently tenable neutral position between these two exists.

If anyone doubts that Modern Theology is really a bottomless abyss of skepticism and despair, let him read the testimony of a seminary professor' who claims:

"I see myself as a typical member of the contemporary seminary community, and I speak not of my own private spiritual condition but of the inward plight of the modern theological sophisticate, wherever he may be found":... Consider the proclamation of my spiritual emancipation. To begin with, I have affirmed my liberation from puritanism.... I say "hell" and "damn" rather more often than is good for the vigor of my English style and enjoy a type of funny story which once was not told in polite company . . . I must confess that my inner life lacks the sense of elation which once characterized the earnest Christian.

I have too many questions about the life of prayer in a world of science, especially in a world so conscious of psychology, to give myself unreservedly to the kind of devotion which ante-dated our present sophistication ... I am also emancipated from Biblicism . . . The old-timers in our churches could give a chapter-and-verse for everything we did and demanded a proof text for every proposed innovation. The Bible was the infallible Word of God, and all man had to do was obey. It is a far cry from this old "cover-to-cover" faith to the knowledge of the Bible which I share with others in the seminary community. The impact of natural science, of evolutionary thought, of historical criticism, of demythologizing, have left us with a Bible utterly unlike the Book our mothers read.

I find that the Bible is still a powerful emotional symbol and that a good many ministers—perhaps even I—resort to a proof text when trying to dragoon reluctant laymen into the support of missions or the practice of tithing . . . While I confess that the passing of the old-line generally recognized authority of the Bible has left popular Protestantism with a gaping hole in its foundations, I must say in all honesty that the old Biblicism is washed up and I cannot seek to

71

revive it.

. . . What now shall I say? As I reflect on my situation, on my emancipation from every characteristic structure of thought in my spiritual heritage, I am shocked into the recognition that every one of these structures has collapsed, at least potentially, and that I stand amid the ruins of every human possibility, even in religion ...

. . . All the old systems, securities, partial explanations are gone. My spiritual pride has departed. I wait alone, a naked, lonely, insecure man among three billion others on a small planet which may be doomed to demolition at any moment or may by great good fortune and the gracious providence of God survive for eons yet to come, spawning billions more like myself, with their own problems, their own insecurities, their own little selves on their hands. For all my destructive wisdom, I am only one of them, standing in icy loneliness and insecurity. Painfully self-conscious, analytical of my every motive, stripped by modern psychology of the possibility of ever acting without devastating reservations and self-doubt, I am left with nothing to trust, no glad cause to espouse, no unsullied banners to march under, no crusade, no historic assurance, no wave of the future.[74]

Toward the end of this tragically unedifying spiritual autobiography (how different from St. Augustine's *Confessions,* for example!), which must be regarded as a damning *testimonium paupertatis* on behalf of Modern Theology, we read this weary irony: "Now perhaps I am ready for the gospel of Christ"!

Even the most militantly "practical" minds must admit that such views as the above have no practical spiritual value whatever. If one has no divine truth to transmit, no real message and comfort from God, but only one's own conjectures, heavily flavored with pseudo-psychological "insights", the work of the Ministry, the Office of the Keys, must indeed be a torture. And so, the same author informs us, the modernistic seminaries, while daring to sneer at the "intellectualism" of the orthodox Church, really prepare their graduates for anything but the Ministry:

The students I observe in seminary, while not wholly comfortable about it, seem to be preparing to become effective builders of the church as an institution, or pastoral counsellors, or professors of theology-if ever there are vast enough faculties to accommodate such an army! [75]

Now, with this whole shocking maze of doubt and uncertainty, forever unregenerately "curved in upon itself", in the vicious circularity of impenitent unbelief, compare the joyful confidence, of Christian Faith, which instructs consciences to "cry for the truth and instruction from God's Word; and to them death is not as bitter as is doubt in any point of doctrine."[76]

Against the sophisticated agnostic Erasmus, Martin Luther wrote, in that book which he himself considered his best :

. . . you say that *you find so little satisfaction in assertions that you would readily take up the Sceptics' position wherever the inviolable*

72

*authority of Holy Scripture and the Church's decisions permit:
though you gladly submit your judgment to these authorities in all
that they lay down, whether you follow it or not* . .. To take no pleasure in assertions is not the mark of a Christian heart; indeed, one
must delight in assertions to be a Christian at all. (Now, lest we be
misled by words, let me say here that by "assertion" I mean
staunchly holding your ground, stating your position, confessing it,
defending it and persevering in it unvanquished ... And I am talking
about the assertion of what has been delivered to us from above in
the Sacred Scriptures...) Away, now, with Sceptics and Academics
from the company of us Christians; let us have men who will assert,
men twice as inflexible as very Stoics! ... Nothing is more familiar
or characteristic among Christians than assertion. Take away assertions, and you take away Christianity . . . What Christian can
endure the idea that we should deprecate assertions? That would
be denying all religion and piety in one breath-asserting that religion and piety and all dogmas are just nothing at all.

. . . The Christian will rather say this: "So little do I like skeptical
principles, that, so far as the weakness of my *flesh* permits, not
merely shall I make it my invariable rule steadfastly to adhere to
the sacred text in all that it teaches, and to assert that teaching,
but I also want to be as positive as I can about those non-essentials
which Scripture does not determine; for uncertainty is the most miserable thing in the world." ... And what Christian would so throw to
the winds the commands of both Scripture and the Church as to say
"whether I follow or not"? . .. Woe to the Christian who doubts the
truth of what is commanded him and does not follow it!—for how
can he believe what he does not follow? . . . The Holy Spirit is no
Sceptic, and the things He has written in our hearts are not doubts
or opinions, but assertions-surer and more certain than sense and
life itself.[77]

Elsewhere Luther wrote:

Whatever wavers or doubts, that cannot be truth. And what would
be the use or need of a Church of God in the world, if she would
waver and be uncertain in her words, or propose something new
every day, now give this, now take that? . . . Doctrine . . . does not
belong into the Our Father when we pray Forgive us our debts! For
doctrine is not of our doing, but it is God's own Word, who cannot
sin nor do wrong. For a preacher must not pray the Our Father, nor
seek forgiveness of sins, when he has preached (if he is a true
preacher), but he must say and boast with Jeremiah, Jer. 17: 16:
"Lord, Thou knowest, that out of my mouth hath gone forth that
which is right and pleasing to Thee", yea, he must defiantly say with
St. Paul and all Apostles and Prophets: *Haec dixit Dominus,* This
God Himself has said. And again: I have been an Apostle and
Prophet of Jesus Christ in this sermon. Here it is not necessary, yea
not good, to ask for forgiveness of sin, as if it were taught wrongly;
for it is God's and not my word, which God neither should nor can

forgive me, but must confirm, praise, crown, and say: You have taught aright, for I have spoken through you and the Word is Mine. He who cannot boast thus of his sermon, let him leave preaching alone, for he surely lies and blasphemes God . . . Life may well be sin and wrong, yea alas it is only too wrong: but *doctrine* must be absolutely straight and certain, without all sin. Therefore in the Church nothing but the certain, pure and only Word of God must be preached. When that is lacking, then it is no longer the Church, but the devil's school.[79]

And the great American *Lutherus redivivus,* Dr. C. F. W. Walther,, wrote, in his classic on the Law and the Gospel:

This thesis divides into two parts. The first part states a requisite of an orthodox teacher, *viz.,* that he must present all the articles of faith in accordance with Scripture. This, in our day, is regarded as an unheard-of demand. Even in circles of so-called believers, people act as if they were shocked when they hear someone say: "I have found the truth; I am certain concerning every doctrine of revelation." Such a claim is considered a piece of arrogance. Young students in particular dare not set up such a claim. In Germany they are told: "Whatever you do, do not believe that you have already found the truth. Keep on studying until you have reached the goal. Never say you have already reached it!"... "Never speak of the Christian doctrine in terms of finality!" They are afraid that someone might speak with finality on an article of faith instead of ceaselessly rolling the stone of research, as Sisyphus in the Greek hell is rolling the stone that he wants to bring to a higher level and which always slips from him. That was the reason, too, why Kahnis, who had been a faithful Lutheran, sought to justify himself in the preface of his miserable *Dogmatik* by citing the Latin proverb *Dies diem docet ...* He meant to say: "A year ago I believed this and that; but other thoughts came to me, and I found other doctrines." That is a miserable; yes an appalling position for a theologian to take .. Scripture requires that we have the Word of God absolutely pure and unadulterated... In our day, men have become merged in skepticism to such an extent that they regard anyone who sets up the afore-mentioned claim: as a semi lunatic ... It is, then, a diabolical teaching to say: "You will never achieve the ability to give a Scriptural presentation of the articles of faith." Especially when students hear a statement like this, it is as if some hellish poison were injected into their hearts; for after that they will no longer show any zeal to get to the bottom of the truth, to have clear conceptions of the truth.[76]

Conclusion

Small-looking mistakes in assumptions have a habit of developing into huge errors in conclusions. An error in first principles soon begets other errors by deduction, so that finally the whole structure becomes permeated with falsehood. Nowhere is this truer than in Theology. Scriptural Theology is being attacked, and mostly in the area of first principles *(Pro-*

legomena). The steady chipping away at the foundations endangers not merely this or that particular doctrine, but the entire structure of Confessional Lutheranism, and thus of historic Christianity.

If Scriptural Theology is to be maintained and defended, it will not do to conduct this defense along arbitrary, shifting, and therefore vulnerable lines. It will not do weakly to defend anemic hybrid positions, or to prop up mechanically the externals, the superstructure, while enemies and false friends are busy destroying the foundations! Any abandonment of the latter in principle abandons the entire fortress, by opening to the enemy a gate which cannot be shut, and through which corrosion will spread like a cancer, till nothing is left, But if the foundations are preserved, all is well, and the fortress remains impregnable. "The Word they still shall let remain!"

It is essential, therefore, that parish pastors and informed laymen, who have not, by constant reading, association and "discussion", been robbed of their capacity for real moral indignation at the enormity of it all, should understand exactly, and in plain words, what is involved, and what destructive assumptions lie hidden beneath all the glitter and glamour of technical verbiage, academic standing, literary charm, elegance, and sophistication, and genuine intellectual labor, which combine to create for Modern Theology an effective illusion of legitimacy.

Orthodox clergy and theologians cannot avoid contact with the fashionable "theology". They may indeed be awed by the achievements of the latter, which, considered as an accumulation of data, are not without merit. The use of this material, by any theologian who wishes to address himself to the modern situation, is inevitable. Nor is that bad. The Church welcomes facts, no matter who points them out. The danger is, however, that unless the greatest caution and discrimination are exercised, not merely facts, but also the surrounding web of assumptions and interpretations will be absorbed from Modern Theology. And the smallest dose of the latter is lethal! There is great danger, for example, that a superficial approach, enthusiastic about the "respectable" status of Modern Theology as an academic discipline, will begin to copy more and more of the latter's methods. One must be keenly aware, therefore, that the methods of Modern Theology have certain hidden assumptions, and therefore cannot simply be taken over by orthodox Theology. Modern theological method, as we have seen, is not a purely formal thing, but an activity which presupposes a definitely anti-Christian world view. Orthodox circles which have begun to employ the methods of Modern Theology, under the illusion that these are purely formal and devoid of inherent and false assumptions, have to that extent no longer been able to produce clear sounds from their trumpets! And this was not simply accidental, or the result of incompetence, but necessary and inevitable.

We may fittingly conclude with a quote which epitomizes the essential difference between Christian Theology and "Modern Theology". Reviewing Dr. F. Pieper's *Christian Dogmatics,* in *The Lutheran Outlook,* organ of the now defunct American Lutheran Conference, G. H. Muedeking severely criticizes Dr. Pieper for his doctrinal rigour and certainty, and then comments: "One travels the old-fashioned roads of religion in this book, when *religion was the dominant interest in life,* and when all opposing ideas were roundly damned, from the Athanasian Creed to some of the documents issuing from the Predestinarian controversy".[80] (Our emphasis). A finer compliment to Dr. Pieper is difficult to imagine! Yes, that is just the point: Christian Theology takes religion seriously; "Modern Theology", in the final analysis, does not!

NOTES:

1. *Christian Century,* vol. LXXI, pp. 1455 ff.

2. Emil Brunner, *Offenbarung und Vernunft* (Zurich: Zwingli-Verlag, 1941) p. 8

3. Ibid., p. 150

4. Ibid., pp. 153-154

5. John Baillie. *The Idea of Revelation in Recent Thought,* (New York: Columbia University Press, 1956, p. 29

6. Ernest Wright, *God Who Acts* (London: SGM Press, 1952) p. 107

7. Robert Preus, "The Word of God in the Theology of Barth." *CTM.,* v.31, no. 2 (February, 1960) p. 109

8. Gustav Aulen, The Faith of the Christian Church (Philadelphia: Muhlenberg Press, 1948) p. 75

9. Ibid., p. 94

10. Gustav Wingren, *Theology in Conflict,* (Philadelphia: Muhlenberg Press, 1958), pp. 3ff.

11. Gordon H. Clark, "The Bible as Truth," *Bibliotheca Sacra;* vol. 114 no. 454 (April, 1957) p. 170

12. David Hedegard, *Ecumenism and the Bible,* (Orebro: Evangeliipress, 1954) pp. 55 ff.

13. Op. *cit.,* pp. 167 ff.

14. Martin H. Scharlemann, *The Bible as Record, Witness and Medium,* p. 12

15. Ibid.

16. G. Wehrung, quoted in the T. Engelder, *Scripture Cannot be Broken,* p. 391

17. Emil Brunner, *Revelation and Reason,* p. 122, n. 9

18. Martin Franzmann, "The New Testament View of Inspiration" CTM, vol. 25, no. 10, Oct. 1954, p. 747.

19. Emil Brunner, *Offenbarung und Vernunft* (Zurich: Zwingli-Verlag, 1941) p. 9, n. 13.

20. Edith Hamilton, *The Greek Way to Western Civilization* (Mentor edition, 1954) p. 208

21. Eric Hoffer, *The True Believer* (Mentor edition, 1958) p. 151

22. Bernard Ramm, *The Pattern of Authority* (Grand Rapids: Eerdmans, 1957) p. 51

23. Martin H. Franzmann, "The Posture of the Interpreter," CTM, vol. 2, no. 3 (March, 1960) p. 158

24. Robert D . Preus, "The Word of God in the Theology of Karl Barth." CTM, vol. 31 no. 2 (February, 1960) p. 113

25. Bengt Haeglund, *Die Heilige Schrift und Ihre Deutung in der Theologie Johann Gerhards* (Lund: Berlingska Boktryckeriet, 1951) p. 78.

26. Emil Brunner, *The Christian Doctrine of Creation and Redemption (Dogmatics,* volume II) p . 328

27. Quoted in Charles Caldwell Ryrie, *Neo-Orthodoxy* (Chicago: Moody Press, 1956) p. 52. This brochure, by the way, is rather good.

28. Quoted in Robert D. Preus, "The Word of God in the Theology of Karl Barth." CTM, vol. 31, no. 2 (February, 1960), pp. 110-111

29. Willis B. Glover, *"The Irrelevance of Theology,"Christian Century,* vol. 76, no. 52 (December 30, 1959) p. 1520

30. David Hedegard, op. cit., p. 57

31. Karl Barth, *Kirchliche Dogmatik,* 1/2, p. 565.

32. Ibid., p. 588

33. Emil Brunner, op. cit., p. 133

34. Ibid., p. 367

35. Charles Caldwell Ryrie, op. cit., pp. 49-50.

36. Chester Tulga, *The Case against Neo-Orthodoxy* (Chicago: Conservative Baptist Fellowship: 1959)

37. Franz Pieper, *Christliche Dogmatik* (St. Louis: Concordia Publishing House, 1924) vol. 1, pp. 77ff. *Lehre und Wehre,* vol. 31, no. 9 (September, 1885) pp. 275 ff. vol. 37, no. 7 (July, 1891) pp. 13 ff., Vol. 37, no. 12 (Dec. 1891) pp. 23 ff.

38. op. cit., p. 240

39. Arnold W. Hearn, "Fundamentalist Renascence," *Christian Century,* (April 30, 1958) pp. 528 ff.

40. Gustaf Wingren, op. cit., p. 125

41. op. cit., p. 91

42. James A. Pike, "Three-pronged Synthesis," *Christian Century,* vol. 77 no. 51 (December 21, 1960) p. 1496

43. J. G. Machen, *Christianity and Liberalism* (New York: Macmillan, 1924) pp. 111-112

44. C. C. Pyrie, op. cit., p. 10.

45. *A Handbook of Christian Theology* (New York: Meridian Books, 1960), pp. 327 ff.

46. *Ibid.,* pp. 258 ff.

47. Editorial in *The Christian Century,* May 21, 1958, p. 611.

48. John Baillie, *The Idea of Revelation in Recent Thought* (New York: Columbia University Press, 1954), p. 115.

49. *Lehre und Wehre,* 1888, p. 196, quoted in *Walther and the Church* (St. Louis: Concordia Publishing House, 1938), p. 14.

50. Quoted *Ibid.*

51. *Concordia Theological Monthly,* January, 1939, p. 65.

52. Vergilius Ferm (ed.), *What is Lutheranism,* p. 279.

53. Francis Pieper, *Christian Dogmatics* (St. Louis: Concordia Publishing House, 1950), vol. I, pp. 296 ff.

54. E. Thestrup Pedersen, *Luther som Skriftfortolker. I. En studie Luthers shriftftsyn, hermeneutik og eksegese* (Copenhagen: 1959).

55. Pieper, *op cit.,* p. 239.

56. *Ibid.*

57. Gustaf Aulen, *The Faith of the Christian Church* (Philadelphia: Muhlenberg Press, 1948), pp. 81-82.

58. Pieper, *op cit.,* p. 229.

59. Papers of the Conference of Theologians, Oakland, California, U.S.A., 1959.

60. Aulen, *op. cit.,* p. 83.

61. Horace Hummel, "Problems of Biblical Interpretation," *Seminarian* (Concordia Seminary, St. Louis, Missouri, U.S.A.), March, 1957, p. 30.

62. *Ibid.,* May, 1957, pp. 37-39.

63. Quoted in *Walther and the Church,* p. 15.

64. *Lutherischer Rundblick,* November, 1959, p. 193.

65. *Concordia Theological Monthly,* March, 1962, pp. 143 ff.

66. *Ibid.,* pp. 143-152.

67. G. K. Chesterton, *Heretics* (London: The Bodley Head, 1960), pp. 295 ff.

68. Aulen, *op. cit.,* p. 19.

69. Alan Richardson, *Creeds in the Making* (London: . SCM Press, 1961), pp. 9-21.

70. H. Hamann, "The Heart of Confessionalism," *Australasian Theological Review,* September, 1956, pp. 61 ff.

71. Arthur Repp, "Teaching the Word to Youth," *Proceedings,* Texas District, The Lutheran Church-Missouri Synod, 1958, pp. 47-48.

72. Pieper, *op.cit.,* pp. 100 ff.

73. *Lehre und Wehre,* Vol. 14, No. 5, p. 135.

74. Ronald E. Osborn, "Up from Emancipation," *The Pulpit,* November, 1960, pp. 7 (327) ff.

75. *Ibid.,* p. 10.

76. *Apology of the Augsburg Confession,* Art. XII, *De Confessione,* 129.

77. Martin Luther, *The Bondage of the Will* (London : James Clarke & Co. Ltd.), pp. 66 ff.

78. Martin Luther, *Wider Hans Wurst,* quoted in C. F. W. Walther, *Die Evangelisch-Lutherische Kirche die Wahre Sichtbare Kirche Gottes auf Erden* (St. Louis: Concordia, 1891), pp. 131 ff.

79. C. F. W . Walther, *The Proper Distinction Between Law and Gospel* (St. Louis: Concordia, 1929), pp. 30 ff.

80. *The Lutheran Outlook,* October, 1950, pp. 311-313.

Christian News, December 16, 1963, May 4, 1964 and September 7, 1964

1. Why is the present crisis in Christendom more radical than previous

ones? ____
2. What is at stake today? ____
3. Today the real issue has to do with the very concept of ____.
4. Today the question should not be ___ but ____.
5. Karl Barth denies the existence of ____.
6. What did Gustaf Aulen and Anders Nygren teach about propositional truth? ___
7. If there is no truth, who is out of business? ____
8. Lundensianism like Barthianism represents ____.
9. When Jesus told the Samaritan woman she told the truth he meant ____.
10. John Baillie wishes to correct ____.
11. The Greeks had no authoritative ____.
12. Barth and neo-orthodoxy are unable to emancipate themselves from ____.
13. Unlike the Bible, Plato and modern theology resort to myth to ____.
14. The Resurrection is for Brunner not ____ but ____.
15. What did Olav Valen Sendstad conclude?____
16. Kant's distinction between the ____ and ____ is basic to the thought of most influential Protestant theologians of the last century and a half.
17. Neo-Orthodoxy is a new and worse form of ____.
18. For Barth the Bible is ____.
19. Tillich may be regarded as ____.
20. The New theology uses all ____ but fills them with ____.
21. Gustaf Aulen denies the ____.
22. What did Bishop James Pike teach about the virgin birth of Christ? ____
23. J. Gresham Machen protested against ____ of the old liberalism.
24. What is the fundamental principle of the truthfulness of language?____
25. What is the Formal Principle of sacred theology?____
26. What determines everything in theology? ____
27. What is Schwaemerei? ____
28. What is the decisive difference between Orthodoxy and Neo-orthodoxy? ____
29. Modern Protestantism says that the Bible __ the Word of God but that it ____ the Word of God.
30. John Baillie denied the ____.
31. Inerrancy is a reliable indicator of ____.
32. What did C.F.W. Walther say about inerrancy? ____
33. What did E. Thestrup Pedersen show about the "liberal" interpretation of Luther? ____
34. The doctrine of the inerrancy of the Bible rests on ____.
35. Does the availability or unavailability of the original manuscripts affect the doctrine of inspiration? ____
36. Inerrancy means a total absence of ____.
37. For Bultmann the resurrection of Christ is a mere ____.

38. What does Tillich say about the existence of a personal God? ___
39. The historical critical method is simply ____.
40. What does the historical critical method say about the authorship of Psalm 110?____
41. All of Scripture is thoroughly ____ and all of it is ____.
42. Has modern research discovered so many new facts about the Bible that new methods of interpretation are needed? ____
43. What is hermeneutics? ____
44. The denatured "Biblical theology" is no longer ____.
45. For the Orthodox Church theology is first of all ____.
46. Christ founded not a discussion club or debating society for the discovery of the truth but a ____ Church for the ____ of the truth.
47. What is absent today from modern theology? ____
48. Paul Tillich has succeeded in refining Christianity to ____.
49. What would be a mistake for orthodox Lutherans? ____
50. Chesterton quipped that no one is more practical in practice that he who is ____ in theory.
51. In the Christian Church ____ is the all important thing.
52. Do Exegesis and Dogmatics represent two conflicting positions? ____
53. Modern theology is a bottomless pit of ____.
54. The Church welcomes ____ regardless of who points them out.
55. Christian theology takes ____ seriously, modern theology ____.

WHAT IS THEOLOGY OR:
IN DEFENSE OF DOGMA

Theology is and must be men of God speaking the Word of God to the people of God. Nowadays it has largely become learned gentlemen writing for learned gentlemen about learned gentlemen.

What has happened is that theology has gone "scientific." Not Scripture but the Scientific Method now has the last word. So sacrosanct has this Method in fact become, that modern "theology" can make do without many things—without an inspired Scripture, a divine Christ, a real Redemption, even without a personal God—but not without the Scientific Method!

This is not to deny that scientific methodology has legitimate uses in the Church. Applied to certain subsidiary issues, particularly in the realm of apologetics, it can be very useful. The point is that it must never be allowed to function as an autonomous principle, determining doctrine, but must restrict itself to such chores as may be assigned to it under the command and strict supervision of the written Word of God, which must always remain in control.

The irrelevance of the Scientific Method as a total principle in theology would be much more obvious, were it not for one persistent illusion. That is the superstitious belief that if allowed to function just a little longer, "scientific" theology will arrive at firm and definite conclusions, which will end the present chaos. Starry-eyed young book-worms at the seminaries, unless otherwise occupied in secular revolutions, wait with bated breath for the latest German research into whatever "theological problem" happens to be "in" that season. The solution seems just around the corner, the "scholarly consensus" just on the point of crystallizing. The church politicians encourage this state of mind, because it enables them to excuse any messy status quo as an almost virtuous but at least unavoidable preliminary stage, which will surely usher in the promised "clarification." Until then all judgments must remain suspended—permanently, it turns out.

For unlike the idealistic youngsters, the wily old statesmen know very well that the solutions never arrive, and the consensus never materializes. Instead, somebody drags a new problem across the trail, and the chase begins afresh.

"Problem" seems in fact to be the basic category of modern theology. To paraphrase Albert Nock on democracy: "Every time one of our first-string publicists opens his mouth, a 'problem' falls out; and every time he shuts it, he bites one in two that was trying to get out."

This inability to attain any sort of stable "assured results" is not accidental, but is inherent in the empirical-scientific approach to theology. In the first place, there is the problem of the "data." In physics or chemistry the matter is quite straight-forward. But what are the "data" of the theology? Scripture, tradition, history, reason, experience? The mutual relation of these aspects depends on a number of basic assumptions which cannot possibly by provided by the Science Method. Mere method, without any substantive principle of authority, cannot possibly produce content, and so becomes "the fleshpot of those who live in metaphysical deserts" (Buckley)[1]. The result is that subjectivism reigns supreme. Every theologian programs the Method with his own assumptions and preferences, and then announced the result as "scientific." If a consensus seems imminent, the threat is soon averted by some enterprising scholar who manages to give the kaleidoscope a slightly different tilt. In classic laissez faire style, there is a constant demand for new fads, and original-ity is rewarded in terms of academic careers. And so the Hegelian tread-mill grinds on. Luther's dictum about scholastic theology ("the one milks the billy-goat and the other holds the sieve") fits modern theology even better. Since Schleiermacher it has been attempting to spin the gold of truth out of the straw of "the ego of the theologizing subject." This means, quite literally, serving the flesh, the "belly" (koilia) of Romans 16:18, in the Hebrew sense of man's interior, the heart, or the seat of mind, will, and feelings. And Original Sin has plenty of "originally," i.e. egotistic in-ventiveness, Is. 53:6!

Secondly, the moment it is agreed that theology must be scientific, in the modern, empirical-descriptive sense, Gustaf Aulen's terrible corollary necessarily follows: "The object of research is an ideal goal toward which theology can only strive in its endeavor to attain to the truth."[2] Science, understood as systematizes generalization based on observed fact, rather than in the classical sense of certain knowledge, always moves toward truth, not from it. Theology so conceived, keeps on groping for an ulti-mate truth which remains always beyond its grasp. No matter what "progress" is made, the horizon, together with the pot of gold at the end of the rainbow, keeps on receding. This really implies that "scientific" theology is a program for avoiding the truth, rather than one for finding it. For that truth must always be sought must mean in practice that it dare never be found. If it were ever found, the whole theological enter-prise would have to grind to a halt. And so the dreary perpetuum mobile keeps on moving, like a revolving door, without ever getting anywhere; Tantalus forever reaching for the unobtainable fruit, Sisyphus ever put-ting his shoulder to the rock that keeps on slipping down!

But Christ never founded a discussion club for the eventual discovery of truth: He founded a teaching church for the proclamation of it, Matt. 28:18ff. For empirical science, truth is the terminus ad quem, the point of arrival; for theology it is the terminus a quo, the starting point. The-ology must announce and apply the truth for man's salvation. For our human, temporal affairs, probabilities, approximations, and provisional truths are quite adequate. But in matters of salvation, nothing less than certain, absolute, final truth will do. "For good consciences cry for the truth and for right instruction from God's Word, and to them death is not as bitter as doubt in any point" (Apology).[3] Unlike Satan ("Yea, hath God said...?" Gen. 3:1) and Pontius ("What is truth?") Pilate, Christ willed that His people should be certain of His word and truth, John 8:32. And in connection with I Tim. 3:15, Dr. F. Pieper said, in one of his great

"Luther Hour" lectures:

> The Christian Church as such deals in nothing but certainty. To the extent that an ecclesiastical fellowship teaches uncertainties, presents doubtful things, or gives rise to doubts, to that extent it does not have the divinely willed character of the Christian Church.[4]

The humanistic, world-wise problem-theology of our time can only smile uncomprehendingly at such language. Playing "science," it neither wants nor offers certainty. For all its clichés about "commitment," "Angst," etc., it is essentially frivolous and fleshly. It is autonomous man speculating leisurely, all the while complimenting himself on his impenitent rebelliousness, fondly imaging it to be proof of his having "come of age!" This is the very quintessence of all "theology of glory."

Let Luther, that great theologian of the Cross, teach us the meaning of Christian certainty:

> Whatever wavers or doubts, that cannot be truth. And what would be the use or need of a Church of God in the world, if she would waver and be uncertain in her words, or propose something new every day, now give this, now take that?...Doctrine...does not belong into the Our Father, nor seek forgiveness of sins when he has preached (if he is a true preacher), but he must say and boast with Jeremiah, Jer. 17:16: "Lord, Thou knowest, that out of my mouth hath gone forth that which is right and pleasing to Thee," yea he must defiantly say with St. Paul and all Apostle and Prophets: Haec dixit Dominus, This God Himself has said. And again: I have been and Apostle Prophet of Jesus Christ in this sermon. Here it is not necessary, yea, not good to ask for forgiveness of sin, as if it were taught wrongly; for it is God's and not my word, which God neither should nor can forgive me, but must confirm, praise, crown, and say: You have taught aright, for I have spoken through you and the Word is Mine. He who cannot boast thus of his sermon, let him leave preaching alone, for he surely lies and blasphemies God...Life may well be sin and wrong, yea alas it is only too wrong: but doctrine must be absolutely straight and certain, without all sin. Therefore in the Church nothing but the certain, pure and only Word of God must be preached. When that is lacking, then it is no longer the Church, but the devil's school.[5]

The peace-loving, mediating theology of the great humanist scholar, Erasmus of Rotterdam, struck Luther as intolerably skeptical. Replying to Erasmus Diatribe, Luther wrote in his *Of the Bondage of the Will*, which he himself considered his best book:

> For it does not befit a Christian heart not to take pleasure in firm assertions, yes it must take pleasure in firm assertions, or else it cannot be Christian. But by "firm assertion" I mean (lest we play with words) steadfastly adhering, affirming, confessing, defending and invincibly maintaining...Let the sceptics and academics be far from us Christians, but let there be in our midst firm assertors, men twice as inflexible as the very Stoics...Nothing is more familiar and usual among Christians than firm assertion. Take away assertions,

and you have taken away Christianity...The Holy Spirit is no Sceptic, and has written into our hearts not doubts or mere opinions, but firm assertions, firmer and more certain than life and sense itself.[6]

So obnoxious was Erasmus' uncertain and compromising theology to Luther's certainty of the Gospel, that the latter was even willing to record in his testament, before witnesses, that he regarded Erasmus "as the great enemy of Christ" in a thousand years.[7]

His basic idea, said Luther, was "that there is no God, therefore he plays so securely in great, serious things, and does not assert, but plays with doubletalk."[8]

Elsewhere Luther teaches: "Our theology is certain, because it causes us not to look to ourselves, but to that which is outside of us, viz., the promise and truth of God."[9] "Into theology and prayer no doubt and uncertainty may fall."[10] "In theology there is neither exception nor exemption, there one must be absolutely certain."[11]

Now, what honest person will dare to maintain that this spirit animates the nominally "Lutheran" theology of our time? Luther's dogmatic certainty, so crucial to the Reformation Faith, is the very thing most bitterly detested and attacked by the Martys and the Pelikans, the Quanbecks and the Sittlers. These devotees of the Zeitgeist tend to portray the Reformation as a perpetual revolution against all established dogmatic positions, with actual sixteenth-century doctrine as a non-essential, time-bound accident, when the Reformation held precisely the opposite view of itself, namely as representing a permanent doctrinal position, accidently in conflict with temporary ecclesiastical conditions. The misrepresentation is serious. That its perpetrators can be accepted as authentic spokesmen for Luther's theology merely illustrates the maxim that the world wants to be deceived and is rarely disappointed!

DOGMA

The great battle for Christian certainty is basically the battle for dogma, doctrine, revealed truth. The whole idea is foreign and repulsive to neology. Modern theology cannot begin until dogma, God-given teaching, has been abolished. Christian theology on the other hand cannot begin without dogma and the Scripture-principle which sustains it.

The neological corrosion has eaten so deeply into our theological mentality, that dogmatics is in very ill repute almost everywhere. It is thought to be a dreary inspection tour through the man-made maze of scholastic subtleties invented by "the dogmaticians," from which the student emerges with a chilled liver and badly in need of a hot cup of "Biblical Theology." Dogmatics is thought to convey mere human tradition and teaching, while Exegesis has a monopoly on Biblical substance, or rather Biblical witness, motifs, concepts, interpretations, insights, stances, and encounters. (There is no dogma!)

This class-warfare interpretation of the relation between dogmatics and exegesis is totally misconceived. Of course a particular dogmatics may conflict with a particular exegesis. But dogmatics and exegesis as such are simply different aspects of the same thing and cannot possibly be in conflict. Dogmatics is essentially content, and exegesis is essentially method. A proper understanding and interpretation of the Bible (exegesis) establishes correct Biblical doctrine (dogmatics). A person who teaches false human ideas in the name of God's Word is not simply a bad exegete, but above all a bad dogmatician. Our age of specialization has led to the superstition that "exegetes" are one set of people and "dogmatician" another, when in actual fact exegesis and dogmatics are but different functions of the same person. A dogmatician who cannot establish his doctrine Biblically is a bad dogmatician, and an exegete who cannot define Biblical doctrine is a bad exegete. Good exegesis and good dogmatics are indivisible.

Dogma, doctrina divina, God's own teaching, is the one integrating factor which holds the four areas of theology, dogmatic, exegetical, historical, and practical, together.

> Dogma is the unifying core of the various theological disciplines. The dogma, the Scriptural doctrine, is the essential element in every discipline, which integrates all branches of sacred theology. The dogmatician must also be an exegete, the historian, and the practical theologian must also be a good dogmatician. Each must be well acquainted with the Scripture doctrine in all its parts.—In spite of the demand for an "undogmatic" Christianity, we declare: "Only dogmatics is edifying," namely, dogmatics as doctrina divina, revealed in Scripture, the only doctrine which may be taught in Christ's Church. In the Christian Church, doctrine is the all-important thing.[12]

Scoffing at dogma and dogmatics may make sense in the Church of the Thirty-Nine Articles or in that of Wesley's Sermons, but never in that Church whose modern historical form was conceived in Theses, born of a Confession, and weaned on a Formula!

This raises the whole matter of creeds and confessions. Can Biblical truth be restated? Do confessional documents purvey divine truth itself, or merely human approximations, interpretations, etc.? What makes confessional statements binding?

A well from which one cannot draw, and a mine which yields nothing, are useless. So is Scripture as the source of doctrine, if it does not actually yield doctrine, but only human approximations and attempts. The whole point of the Reformation's Scripture principle is that clear, certain divine truth is directly available for teaching and faith. Luther simply equates "doctrine" with "God's Word." Concrete teaching taken from Scripture, however formulated, is God's own Word, truth, and doctrine. The Lutheran Church in her official Confessions takes the same stand. They claim to represent not aspects, interpretations, views, emphases, etc., but "the pure unhallowed, and unadulterated light of his holy Gospel," the "right course of divine truth," the "divine truth that our pious forebearers and we have acknowledged and confessed."[13] Subscription to the Confessions in any other sense is contrary to their original intention and therefore fraudulent.

The modern habit of speaking of the Confessions as "response" to God's revelation is very misleading. It changes God-given doctrine into a human construct and suggests the Platonic scheme of earthly, concrete formulations trying their best to express correctly the absolute truth (the transcendent Ideas!), but necessarily, of course, the moderns regard Scripture itself as being not divine revelation regard Scripture itself as being not divine revelation itself, but merely a human "response" or "witness" to it. On the other hand, they are being strangely inconsistent when they insist (1) against "Fundamentalism" that not only Scripture but also Biblical preaching is the Word of God, (2) with "Fundamentalist" anti-creedalism that doctrinal formulations cannot be the Word of God!

But the quicksand of a false conservatism is even more deadly than the honest abyss of modernist denial. I refer to that attitude which thinks it can safely compromise Biblical authority and inerrancy, and then use the Confessions as antidote to keep the corrosive poison within bounds. But this is like rescuing the sun by means of the moon, or building the foundation on the house, rather than the other way round. The Confessions presupposes the Scriptures as unshakable foundations. Remove these, and the superstructure must collapse as well.

When the Reformation's Scripture principles is surrendered, a Romanizing view of the Church and of tradition must be resorted to, to prop up the tottering Confessions. Consider Elert's statements that the doctrine of the Trinity is "a dogma which presupposes beside the Scripture also the ancient Church as source."[14] If this means anything at all, it means that the doctrine of the Trinity cannot be established from the Scriptures alone, but that the Nicene Creed, etc., must come to the rescue. This would mean, however, that the Trinity it a non-Biblical and therefore non-Christian doctrine, a mere human invention, and a piece of ecclesiastical traditionalism. Yet Nicaea accepted the Creed not on its own authority, but only because it was convinced that the Creed's doctrinal content was "according to the Scriptures."

This plays into the matter of "Open Questions." Some people imagine that only what is explicitly settled in the Confessions can be regarded as binding doctrine. Everything else is an "open question." Consider this blatant formulation from Australian Lutheran history:

> Truths contained or indicated in Scripture, concerning which we as Lutherans who take their stand upon Scripture and Confessions have not as yet attained a unanimous understanding, which moreover, are not considered justifying severance of church-fellowship... we denote as "Open Questions."[15]

This implies (1) that anything on which nominally Lutheran theologians begin to disagree thereby becomes an "open question," and (2) that not Scripture, but the Church, through her Confessions, makes doctrines. Logically this would mean that the Real Presence, for example, was not a doctrine prior to its definition by the Augsburg Confession in 1530, then was one until Luther's death, when "Lutherans who 'claimed to' take their stand upon Scripture and Confessions" disagreed about it, again became a doctrine through Article VII of the Formula of Concord, but today is no longer a doctrine because many "Lutherans" who pay lip-service to the Confessions, reject the Real Presence and fraternize with the Calvinistic churches. I do not say that this was intended by the above formulation, but this is what it clearly allows. (The anomaly was corrected, by the way, in our Theses of Agreement, which clearly state that "all doctrines of Holy Writ are equally binding" (I/4) and that no differences, even in Bible interpretation, may be tolerated if they in any way impair the teaching of Scripture and Confession.)

I know of no better formulation of the correct principle here than Dr. F. Pieper's, written on behalf of the entire Synodical Conference of North America:

> All doctrines revealed in Holy Scripture are to be accepted and believed, for the very reason that they are propounded in Holy Scripture, no matter whether "decided" in the Symbolical Books and agreed upon by the theologians or not. To declare doctrines revealed in the Bible to be "open" or "free" for the reason that they are not yet "symbolically fixed" in the Confessions of the orthodox Church, or not yet accepted by all orthodox theologians, would, in fact, be the same as to put the Church, her Confessions and theologians, in the place of Holy Scripture, and to ascribe to the Church and her theologians the authority of establishing articles of faith.[16]

This is precisely the official position of the Lutheran Church in her Confessions: "the Word of God shall establish articles of faith and no one else, not even an angel."[17] Luther writes: "Let them scream themselves into a frenzy crying 'Church, Church!'—without God's Word it is nothing!"[18] And in the very first of his thirty-eight theses on the authority of the Church (1530), he says: "The Christian Church has no power to establish any article of faith, has never established one, and will nevermore do so."[19] Neither, says Luther, does the Church "confirm" articles of faith, as with a higher or adjudicatory power (the papistic notion), but is itself confirmed by God's Word and doctrine. The only sense in which the church attests or confirms Scripture and the articles of faith, is "as the subject, that it, she recognizes and confesses them, as a slave the seal of his Master" (Thesis 7).

All this is actually relevant to the current discussions in various parts of the world about the status of confessional documents of more recent times.

When the Missouri Synod's 1962 Convention in Cleveland repealed as unconstitutional the previous convention's (San Francisco, 1959) "Resolution 9," which had demanded that the public teachers of the Church teach in harmony with its official doctrinal pronouncements, including the Brief Statement, the St. Louis Lutheran explained, with evident approval:

> Declaration of the resolution as unconstitutional did not alter the Missouri Synod's doctrinal stand but removed its binding force.[20]

But a "doctrinal stand" without "binding force" is neither Biblical, nor Confessional, nor even honest. It is the play-doctrine of frivolous people playing church! Serious confession speaks another language. The Preface to the Book of Concord says:

> These "false and seductive doctrines and their stiff-necked proponents and blasphemers" we do not by any means intend to tolerate in our lands, churches, and schools, inasmuch as such teachings are contrary to the expressed Word of God and cannot coexist with it... our disposition and intention has always been directed toward the goal that no other doctrine be treated and taught in our lands, territories, schools, and churches than that alone which is based on the Holy Scriptures of God and is embodied in the Augsburg Confession and its Apology, correctly understood, and that no doctrine be permitted entrance which is contrary to these...We likewise propose to cooperate with one another in the future in the implementation of this effort at concord in our lands...through diligent visitation of churches and schools, the supervision of printers, and other salutary means.[21]

Luther on I Peter 4:11:

> If anyone speak, that he speaks it as God's Word: that is a very necessary doctrine in the Church...For in Christendom things are not done as in worldly government and affairs...for there is here a spiritual government of consciences before God, and what is here spoken, taught, commanded or done, must happen in such matter that one knows that if is valid and stands before God, yes that it comes and flows from Him, so that one can say: This God Himself has said or done...For it is not to be tolerated that doctrine is treated as it pleases everyone, or seems good and fine to him, or that it is to be arranged to fit human reason and understanding, or that people play and juggle with Scripture and God's Word, so that it would have to let itself be interpreted, steered, stretched, and mended for the sake of people or of peace and unity; for then there would be no certain nor firm foundation, on which consciences could rely.[22]

To proclaim one thing as true and another thing as binding is legalistic church politics. Evangelical theology confesses nothing without being convinced that it is Biblical; but whatever is confessed to be Biblical is thereby self-evidently declared to be binding.

Very startling was the argumentation which convinced the Cleveland Convention to repeal San Francisco "Resolution 9." What was denied was not the merit of any particular doctrinal statement, but the Synod's right to adopt any binding doctrinal statements, since this in effect amended the unalterable doctrinal paragraph of the Synod's constitution which lists only the documents compromising the Book of Concord!

Poor C. F. W. Walther! Little did he realize that he was violating the constitution of the Synod he had founded when in 1881 he caused the "Thirteen Theses" to be adopted (as binding of course), thus settling the Predestination Controversy! Not even his opponents at that time, however, were so incompetent theologically as to deny the Church's right to formulate Biblical truth afresh, in response to current controversies.

Behind the mask of the new piety toward "the Scriptures and the Confessions," which purports to defend the latter against sacrilegious innovations, there lurk rank formalism, legalism, and skepticism. Bible and Confessions are seen formalistically as magic word-patterns, rather than as doctrinal content, meaning, substance, which can and must be restated. This "cow's eye" view is both too strict and too loose: Too strict because it forbids the Church to confess, in case of conflicting interpretations, what it means by its doctrinal formulations, and too loose because it allows anybody and everybody without let or hindrance to connect their own sense or nonsense with the words of the Confessions, thereby defeating their purpose. Henceforth the Confessions are no longer regarded as actual doctrine, which can be ascertained, defined, applied, etc., but only as a "doctrinal basis," which anyone may twist this way or that as he pleases, like a waxen nose!

> In other words, any heretic could teach whatever he pleased, Calvinism, Romanism, or Liberalism, so long as he would claim that he was merely "interpreting" the Scriptures and the Confessions— which is, of course, exactly what these gentry always claim to be doing! And the Synod would be helpless, for the moment it would try to insist on any particular interpretation of Scripture and/or Confession, no matter how obvious, this would be "unconstitutional!" This view of the Scriptures and the Confessions not as doctrinal substance, which a Synod can and must define, defend, and restate as circumstances require, but rather as empty, and very elastic verbal bags which anyone may stuff with whatever content he wishes, is , or course, the very heart, soul, and essence of unionism.[23]

The best refutation of the "cow's eyes," which see new documents and think they see new doctrines, is the Formula of Concord itself. Although it certainly spells out its doctrinal content in much more detail than does the Augsburg Confession, the Formula vehemently denies that it is expanding the doctrinal scope of the Confession in the slightest. It insists on being nothing more—not less!—than the correct understanding of the Augsburg Confession over against various false interpretations. Moreover, the entire Book of Concord as such claims to be not a complete dogmatics, but only a series of doctrinal decisions—Biblical in content, ecclesiastical in form—on controverted articles.[24] Although the Catechisms cover the "chief parts" of the Christian religion, and although the Augsburg Confession and, for instance, Art. XI of the Formula of Concord, deal briefly also with uncontroverted articles, the great bulk of the Concordia is controversial in origin.

Moreover, in the current chaotic state of world "Lutheranism" it is important to remember that practically the entire Formula of Concord was directed not against Rome or Geneva as such, but against false Lutherans, who claimed to be loyal to the Augsburg Confession! Far from accepting the lip-service and declaring the differences intramural, the Formula is determined "to insure that familiar terminology may not hide and conceal something,"[25] and insists that:

> These controversies are not, as some may think, mere misunderstandings or contentions about words, without one party talking

past the other, so that the strife reflects a mere semantic problem of little or no consequence. On the contrary, these controversies deal with weighty and important matters, and they are of such a nature that the opinions of the erring party cannot be tolerated in the church of God, much less, be excused and defended.[26]

Nor does the Book of Concord see itself as a closed canon. The last sentence of the Preface says: "If the current controversies about our Christian religion should continue or new ones arise, we shall see to it that they are settled and composed in timely fashion before they become dangerously widespread in order that all kinds of scandal might be obviated."[27]

Well, "new ones" have arisen in the last four hundred years, as was to be expected. Is the Church now to be gagged because not everything could be anticipated by the Confessions? Here a false conservatism is radical Liberalism's most effective front!

Today's differences about Scripture and the Church, to name the two focal points of the controversy, move on a vastly grander scale than anything settled by the Formula of Concord. Moreover, they have been "dangerously widespread" for a long time, and there has been plenty of "all kinds of scandal." At the same time the debate seems to have reached the repetitious stage, with nothing really new being said by either side, so that, all attempts at making gold and clay hang together having failed, clear-cut alternatives have crystalized. The time seems ripe for great Confessional decisions. The specifics of whether and when and how are of course known to God alone. We can at least, however, identify an obstacle that stands in the way: that blind faith in visible institutions, seminaries, etc., which is a species of what Luther called the "collier's faith"[28] ("I believe what the Church believes! What's that? What I believe!") If we wait for the agreement of all formerly orthodox quarters, we shall wait till doomsday and never confess anything. And if we make the goat the gardener, we shall never harvest anything. Or, as Luther says in another place:

> Perhaps they will palm off on you before the simple people and other undiscerning persons the claim that they have not yet been recognized by the Church as wolves and false teachers, but are considered true Christians. Yes, indeed, that is wisely and well spoken: if the sheep were not to flee from the wolves until the wolves through their Christian Council and public verdict commanded the sheep to flee, then the sheepfold would soon be empty, and the Shepherd would within one day find neither milk, cheese, butter, wool, flesh, nor even a hoof![29]

Nor will it do to borrow the architectural "split-level" concept, and to construct doctrinal statements like terraced hanging gardens, with descending degrees of certainty and authority. What is needed is a clear and binding confession or revealed divine truth in our time and circumstances, "for if the trumpet gives an uncertain sound, who shall prepare himself to the battle?" (I Cor. 14:8)

Before leaving the area of dogmatic or systematic theology, we must examine, however, briefly, an ingeniously camouflaged assault-route into the very heart of Christian doctrine. To all appearance the whole thing is but an abstruse discussion of fine philosophical points. When the average Christian hears that what is being rejected is merely something "metaphysical" or "ontological," he isn't worried at all. He may even mutter, "good riddance," since such terms seem to have nothing to do with the Gospel, and even conjure up negative associations like "philosophy and vain deceit," and "science falsely so called." But when the philosophical cover is thoroughly "defoliated," a very different picture emerges.

> "We need a new Christianity based on entirely new concepts and terms"...
> Numerous theologians, including Lutheran Jaroslav Pelikan and Roman Catholic layman Leslie Dewart, have argued that Christianity must find substitutes for the Greek ideas that have been its philosophical foundation since St. Paul and the Gospel of John.[30]

These sentiments, incidentally, are alleged to be those not of some *Playboy* Freudologian, but of (of all people!) the Greek Orthodox Primate of North and South America, Archbishop Iakovos! Note that the "philosophical foundation" being attacked is explicitly blamed on St. Paul and St. John, not on any sort of medieval scholasticism!

Joseph Sittler has argued, in "A Christology of Function" ("dynamic functions" are "in," "static essences," "out"!), that the classic Christology of the Creeds is based on philosophical ideas which are not relevant in our times, and should be replaced with more modern notions. For example, the idea that Christ existed as a Person from all eternity, prior to the Incarnation, is alleged to be such a dated philosophical notion. The same goes for the whole idea of "two natures" being united in Christ. All this is to be replaced with the more congenial "concept" alleged to be "Hebrew," that Christ never existed as a Person until He was born, except in the sense that God foreknew this single-natured human being from all eternity!

What Malcolm Muggeridge observes about the concept of God holds true of modern theology generally:

> Nietzsche, no Liberal, announced that God was dead; the same Deity's Liberal ministrants today seek to confute Nietzsche by stuffing an empty skin with Freudian entrails.[31]

Similarly all the great Christian terms and doctrines are being emptied of their original meaning and content, under the pretext of removing antiquated philosophy or "mythology." The Resurrection of Christ was not an actual event, but simply the "meaning" of the Crucifixion! The Virgin Birth is mere legendary embellishment, though it "means" something or other. The Incarnation is but an accommodation to ancient Middle-Eastern "thought-forms." In other words, Christian theology is left holding empty verbal bags, all content and meaning having been thrown out as "philosophy." Whenever modern theology begins to huff and puff about anything "metaphysical" or "ontological" it is nearly always an infallible sign that a Christian doctrine is being robbed of its reality, and replaced by some flat, painted "interpretation!"

90

Let a final example illustrate the point. The official Report of the Department of Theology, submitted to the Helsinki (1963) Assembly of the Lutheran World Federation, contained these statements:

> The main concern of the ancient confessions is not metaphysics but soteriology. The statements about the pre-existence of Christ and the Trinity are nothing more than interpretations of the basic soteriological statement "God was in Christ for our salvation."[32]

Being interpreted, in the light of current theological usage, the meaning of these assertions in plain English is about this: The main concern of the ancient confessions was not any particular view of the relation between Christ and God, but salvation. The statements about the pre-existence of Christ and the Trinity are not doctrines in their own right, but merely attempts to explain, in terms of the ideas of those times, some aspects of the basic statement "God was in Christ for our salvation." Today this statement may have to be interpreted quite differently, perhaps by saying that God is not a personal Being at all, but the Ground of Being, and that Jesus Christ "saves" us by showing us the meaning of authentic humanity or existence—without any sort of life beyond the grave of course!

When orthodox quarters resist this process of evisceration, they are generally accused of "rationalism." Suddenly the opponents of Scripture truth are playing the part of loyal defenders of "Biblical thought-forms," while the orthodox are cast in the invidious role of Procrustean humbugs, forcing Scripture to fit into their pre-conceived schemes! The farce is abetted by a certain unhelpfully naïve "exegetical" approach which is content to be allowed to play with word-studies and "imagery," but shies away from serious questions of substance and definition. This know-nothing pseudo-Biblicism accepts unexamined and at face value any package wrapped in "Biblical language," and is insulted if anyone suggests an actual inspection of the contents.

Since the neologists treat Biblical statements as impressionistic word-sketches, they naturally object to any suggestions that these statements convey precise logical content and can sustain rigorous argumentation. This would be "Aristotelian logic," and that is Original Sin! Yet Christ Himself teaches us to treat Scripture with the utmost logical respect and rigor. St. Mat. 22:31-32, 41-45.

> With reference to logical forms our Lord used *Analogy*, Luke, xi. 13; *Reductio Ad Absurdum*, Matt. xii. 26; *Excluded Middle*, Matt. xii. 20; *A Fortiori*, Matt. xii. 1-8; *Implication*, Matt. xii. 28; and *Law of Non-Contradiction*, Luke vi. 39.[33]

The fact of the matter is of course that Holy Scripture, precisely because it is given in human language (this stress on the Bible's humanity ought to endear the argument to the neologists!) necessarily pre-supposes those logical principles, like the law of non-contradiciton, without which no meaningful human discourse is possible. For example, "The Word was made flesh" is a meaningless statement unless we assume, on the basis of the law of non-contradiction, that it means to rule out as false its opposite, viz., "The Word was not made flesh." Again, there is no Scripture-text which says: "'This is My Body' is a logical proposition and therefore rules out its opposite." But unless this is assumed, the Lord's words are senseless. The Bible clearly intends to make sense, and therefore shares the general logical assumptions underlying all human speech. Deny the law of non-contradiction, and every statement means the same as its opposite. But when its meaning has been assassinated, the Bible is fit only to be thrown away.

All this, incidentally, has nothing whatever to do with paradoxes, of which Scripture and the Christian Faith are full. To say, for example, that whoever will lose his life will save it, and vice versa, is not a contradiction, but a paradox. The "losing" and the "saving" are clearly meant in different senses or respects. As a contradiction the statement would be nonsensical and pointless; as a paradox it is a striking formulation of a profound truth.

And speaking of paradox, is it not ironic that the very people who use human reason with a vengeance, magisterially, to judge, correct, and otherwise bully Scripture, complain bitterly of "rationalism," when others wish merely to use logic ministerially, instrumentally, to apprehend what Scripture is saying? It is like the wolf accusing the lamb downstream of muddying the waters! As intelligible communication Scripture is addressed to man through his mind, and is apprehended either intellectually or not at all (I Cor. 14:6 ff.)! And the essentials of logic are not arbitrary conventions, but are inherent features of our Logos-created and Logos-center universe (St. John 1:1 ff). Aristotle invented logic no more than Linlaeus invented the plants he classified!

Nor did Luther reject "Aristotelian logic," as is often asserted. What he rejected was Aristotle's positive philosophy, "since the miserable man teaches in his best book, de anima, that the soul is mortal together with the body."[34] (On this point modern theology is solidly Aristotelian!) But Luther specifically approved of Aristotle's "Logica Rhetorica, Poetica."[35] At Worms Luther was willing to be convinced "by the testimony of Scripture or...by manifest reasoning."[36] See also Bengt Haegglund's illuminating discussion of that truth, reason, Aristotelianism, etc.[37] The much-advertised contrast between Luther and Lutheran Orthodoxy on this point is parallel to the alleged conflict of the ancient creeds: equally plausible, and equally false!

While philosophy, no longer the handmaid of theology, has become "the charwoman of science" (Copleston), theology has become mystical and anti-intellectual. Precision and definitions go against its grain. Demands for doctrinal definitions are scorned as attempts to "prove," "demonstrate" or "explain" divine mysteries rationally. As if stating a mystery were the same as solving it! And how could something be known to be a mystery, unless it could first be stated? Faith may not understand the HOW of the great mysteries, like the Trinity, the Incarnation, the Atonement, the Real Presence, Inspiration, and so on, but it must be able to state clearly the THAT of these articles to believe them at all. What I cannot define, I cannot believe either. If to the question, "What is the Real Presence?" I can only reply "I do not know," then I cannot honestly claim to believe that doctrine. No matter how mysterious the "how," the "what" or "that" must be clear if faith is not to be "collier's faith" and superstition! This means that orthodox, Biblical theology can afford to speak clearly, calmly, and rationally about great, supernatural mysteries, while modern theology, for all its contrived, tricky, and mustifying language, purveys cold, rationalistic dead weight!

As the religious satrapy of modern anti-intellectual Liberalism, current theology descends upon the mind with the obfuscating effect of a huge, slimy cobweb. Though its anti-logical bias makes this stultifying obscurantism as difficult to oppose as the plot of Cymbeline, of which Dr. Johnson observed that it was impossible to criticize unresisting imbecility, it must be resolutely fought off with a "confident intellectualism expressive of robust faith in God, Whose Word is truth."[38] Or, as Dr. Nagel once put it, referring to the late Msgr. Ronald Knox:

> In the smoke-filled contemporary dialectic and abstruse humbug a keen gust of Knoxian clarity is most bracing. "Orthodox theology is not easily intelligible, for on the face of it, it passes man's understanding. But however difficult it may be to fathom, it can be stated on a half-sheet of note-paper."[39]

Modern theology has with much fanfare rehabilitated the body (just in time for the New Morality, thank you!). Will it ever dare to do the same for the mind?

EXEGETICAL, HISTORICAL, AND PRACTICAL THEOLOGY

"Exegesis" which does not subserve faith and teaching is a barren fig-tree and will wither away (St. Matt. 21:19). Of this nature is the approach which wants to abandon historic Christian doctrines, but has nothing definite to put in their place. To show merely what the Bible may possibly mean, is not enough, as Luther often reminds us. Faith needs not uncertain speculations, but a firm text, with a clear meaning, for its foundation. Against Zwingli, Oecolampadius, and their followers, Luther writes, in his great Confession of the Supper of Christ:

> If now there were a true spirit with them, he would not only take away the false understanding, but give and prove another, certain, and truthful one in its stead. If St. Paul had in the most powerful way removed the righteousness of the Law or of works he would of course not have accomplished anything, unless he had also taught and made certain another righteousness in its place. God did not abolish the Old Covenant until He instituted the New Covenant and made it much more certain than the Old.
>
> It is not a fine spirit which teaches and says: This is a lie, and still does not given any certain truth in this place. It won't do to accuse something of being a lie, and not know nor want to show against it her who brings the accusation, the truth. He who wants to smash lies mightily, must in their stead place public, certain, and firm truth; for the lie neither fears nor flees until the bright, firm truth comes...Who can criticize injustice if he does not prove what justice is? It is always the light that must refute the darkness: one

93

darkness does not refute another; so also Beezlebub drives out no devils. This the fanatical spirit feels very well, therefore it stalks about like the cat around the hot porridge, makes a terrible noise about our text and understanding not being right, but shies and flees like the devil before the Word of God, that he won't have to prove that his text and understanding are right; for he feels very well that he can't do it.

Therefore he thinks one should leave it at that, that he abolishes the text of the Lord's Supper according to our understanding, and places no other certain "text and understanding" in its place; no that won't do. If you want to break down, then also build up. If you want to warn of error, then also teach the certain truth in its place, or else leave mastering and teaching alone. For thereby you admit your own defeat, that you are a false, lying spirit, because you scold as false that the opposite of which you cannot and will not make true and certain. But the Holy Spirit knows very well how to prove and make certain the contrary, when He refutes lies or error.[40]

As regards historical theology, it dare not be a non-judgmental, "objective" chronicle of views and events, but it must be, as Luther called it, an account of how the dear Gospel has fared in the world. The historical theologian must take a stand, approving some positions, and condemning others. When Christ asked His disciples about the various "schools of thought" in respect to Himself, He was not satisfied with a mere enumeration of "some say this and some say that." He wanted no discussion, but confession: "Thou are the Christ, the Son of the living God!" (St. Matt. 16).

Dr. A. Hoenecke, in his magnificent historical review of Lutheran theology, calls attention to the fact that to the "so-called historicizing dogmaticians...some dogmatic materials appeared no longer as a received heirloom to be energetically maintained, but more as the object of historical reporting."[41] Classic Lutheran theology rejoiced confidently "in the greatness of the gift of God given in theology, as well as in the infallibility of the source producing it (Scripture as principle of theology)...Everything is in the tone of certainty. Already in the prolegomena Lutheran theology shows itself to be resting securely on Scripture, in faith. There is no arguing, discussing, disputing, and speculating, viz., about epistemology, etc., in order thus to reach certain results, standpoints, and principles."[42] Later things are very different:

> The way which was not taken in the first period, viz., the attempt for instance to obtain the standpoint of Reformation dogmatics by means of a criticism of scholastic dogmatics, was just the way taken in the second period. And that is also the way of the newer theology, i.e. to obtain the right starting point and necessary standpoint of one's own theology by means of criticism of the preceding theology, and through the appropriation of the so-called aspects of truth contained in it.[43]

This sort of application of the objective Gospel as standard and criterion to the history of the Church is historical theology at its best.

It is in practical theology that the whole discipline comes to fruition and achieves its aims. This is theology par excellence. Divine truth was given not for idle speculation, but for salutary application, for the creation and edification of the Church, for the transmission of divine Life for the salvation of men (Eph. 4).

Imagine a hospital without standards. Anyone may practice "medicine" in this hospital as he sees fit. Genuine physicians, quacks, mystics, Christian Scientists, abortionists, and just plain cranks, all serve on equal terms. All points of view may be expressed and practice, but none may be enforced. Among those in very responsible positions, even teaching in the local medical school, are some who have written books denying the existence (1) germs, (2) disease, (3) people. The widest variety of courses is available, depending on who happens to be on duty at the time. One treats pneumonia with X-rays, another mends broken bones with meditation, a third advocates amputation of the head for asthma. Anyone complaining of any form of treatment is reminded of the complete freedom of the hospital and its staff to prescribe any treatment whatsoever, so long as the practitioner in question is sincere. Some doctors do not even make a pretense of curing, but use patients purely as guinea-pigs for scientific experiments. Others spend their time herding patients onto the streets to demonstrate for various social and political causes.

Such a madhouse is of course unthinkable in any civilized country. But change the medical milieu to the theological, and the nightmare becomes instant, reality. For in much of what passes for the Church nowadays, the right of the "theologian" to freedom of belief, expression, research, and what not, and the bureaucrat's right to be a bureaucrat take precedence, as a matter of course, over the ordinary person's right to be told the truth of God's Word and to be spiritually helped.

The medical profession's code and discipline no doubt are among the strictest in all human enterprises, and this despite the fact that medical science is not a revealed absolute, but an imperfect, growing body of knowledge with room for honest disagreements. The theoretical basis for this strictness is the fundamental assumption that the patient's right to be healed must come before all other considerations. It is this, and not mere professional pride or vested interests (which in any case must justify themselves in terms of prior principles) which will prevent a doctor from co-operating or "taking turns" with medically unrecognized quacks and their organizations. Now, if the world can show such respect for the mere biological life of man, and can enforce tentative, imperfect medical science with such rigour, should one not expect the Church to stand in even greater awe of man's supernatural life, which is infinitely more precious, and to fight incomparably greater zeal for the exclusive sway of that absolute, unchanging, revealed divine truth with which she has been entrusted and equipped? But alas, such attitudes are rare. The modern "Church" and modern "theology" are absurdly loose and permissive even from a secular, not to speak of a spiritual point of view. What Malcolm Muggeridge says of the British situation is only too typical:

"the true Doctrine of the Church of England agreeable to God's

Word,"...which few of the bishops and clergy...any longer ever pretend to believe, though all have solemnly assented to them to become ordained.

A ribald scene indeed. Who would ever suppose that a secular enterprise so conducted could possibly thrive or, for that matter, be permissible? Current professional and even business standards would preclude acceptance of a salaried post on the strength of a consciously fraudulent declaration.[44]

Unlike doctors, modern clergy and "theologians" fraternize with anyone and anything. There is no horror of heresy or spiritual quackery, and no ostracism of its representatives, because there is grave doubt whether anyone can really know the truth. There is therefore no way of distinguishing truth from fantasy! Theology and ecclesiology have become Deistic: God is not supposed to care about those details. What Dr. C. F. W. Walther wrote in the last century is still applicable today, only more so:

It has always been not so much the pure doctrine per se, which has aroused hostility against its representatives, much less is that case in our indifferentistic age; but taking it seriously, the exclusive adherence to it, the rejection and condemnation of the opposite doctrine, and above all the practical implementation of this doctrinal position, that it was which at all times provoked hostility...So also the Cardinal of Salzburg said that Luther's doctrine "he would tolerate, but to allow oneself to be reformed out of a corner, that was not to be tolerated." So it still is today. What doctrine isn't one prepared to tolerate nowadays, if only it will stand peacefully beside the other doctrine! And just those who want to be orthodox accomplish the most incredible feats in this tolerance. Only observe the harmonious relation, which shows itself in the academic colleges, the peaceable sitting together in pastoral conferences, the tone in the reviews! [45]

Let Bishop St. Fulgentius teach us the true honor of our theological calling. He was much-persecuted and banished for his loyalty to the Nicene Creed, and had been betrayed by an Arian priest to the Numidians, who had tortured him savagely, plucked out hair and beard, and left him wounded and bleeding. Ashamed of such brutality, the Arian bishop offered to punish his priest, if Fulgentius would prosecute. Did our Confessor agree? Or did he perhaps found an Ecumenical Society for the prevention of Cruelty to Clergymen (co-operation in externals!)? No! With a magnificent sense of the dignity of his Christian faith, calling, and office, he replied: "A Christian must not seek revenge in the world. God knows how to right his servants' wrongs...*and it would be a scandal to many little ones that a catholic, however unworthy he may be, should seek redress from an Arian bishop!*"

And at Augsburg in 1530, when the Elector of Saxony was intimidated with the loss of his lands and people, if he continued to adhere to the Augsburg Confession, he replied that he would rather let go of lands and people than of God's Word. If only we theologians, of whom more is required, had half the interior contempt for careers, official favor, tenure, etc., which that Christian prince had for temporal possessions!

Theology is the Spirit-given ability to apply Law and Gospel, Word and Sacrament, to human beings for their salvation. This sacrament art is supremely practical, hence all true theology must push, with an irresistible interior urgency, toward application and implementation in actual Church life. It is not enough to exchange esoteric academic memoranda, even if their content happens to be orthodox. True theology must be realized in ecclesiastical action, or else it is a fraud. The greater the difficulties, the less we may rely on human wisdom and schemes (St. Matt. 15:9; 16:23), but must cling alone to the Word and promise of Him "who also hath made us able ministers of the new testament" (2 Cor. 3:6). And our Ascended Lord, Who shares with us the spoils and victory of his Resurrection, will invincibly, sustain His cause through that divine Defender Who has never lost a case, and who will "reprove the world of sin, and of righteousness, and of judgment" (St. John 16:18)!

Footnotes

1. William F. Buckley, *Up from Liberalism* (New York: Arlington House, 1968), p. 149.

2. Gustaf Aulen, *The Faith of the Christian Church* (Philadelphia: Muhlenberg, 1948) p. 19.

3. *Apology*, XII, 129, in Die Bekenntnisschriften Der Evangelisch- Lutherischen Kirche (Goettingen: Vandenhoeck & Ruprecht, 1952), p. 279.

4. F. Pieper, *Vortraege Ueber Die Evangelisch Lutherische Kirche, Die Wahre Sichtbare Kirche Gottes Auf Erden* (St. Louis: Seminary Press, 1916), pp. 145-146.

5. Martin Luther, *Saemmtliche Schriften* (St. Louis edition), XVII, 1340 ff.

6. *Ibid.*, XVIII, 1675 ff.

7. *Ibid.*, XXII, 1081.

8. *Ibid.*, XXII, p. 1850.

9. *Ibid.*, IX, 509.

10. *Ibid.*, XXII, 1020.

11. *Ibid.*, p. 1507.

12. F. Pieper, *Christian Dogmatics* (St. Louis: Concordia, 1950), vol. 1, p. 101.

13. Preface to the book of Concord, in Theodore G. Tappert, ed., *The Book of Concord* (St. Louis: Concordia, 1959), pp. 3 ff.

14. W. Elert, *Morphologie Des Luthertums*, p. 160.

15. Theodor Hebart, *Die Vereinigte Ev.-Luth. Kirche In Australien* (Adelaide: Lutheran Book Depot, 1938), p. 283.

16. *The Distinctive Doctrines and Usages of the General Bodies of the Evangelical Lutheran Church in the United States* (Philadelphia: Lutheran Publication Society, 1902), 3rd edition, pp. 139-140.

17. Tappert, ed., OP. CIT., p. 295.

18. St. Louis edition, XII, 1414.

19. *Ibid.*, XIX, 953.

20. *St. Louis Lutheran*, July 7, 1962.

21. Tappert , ed., OP CIT., pp. 11, 12, 14.

22. St. Louis edition, XII, 615 ff.

23. Parish Education Committee, Queensland District, Evangelical Lutheran Church of Australia, Crossroads (Toowoomba, 1965), p. 20.

24. Tappert, ed., OP CIT., p. 6.

25. *Ibid.*, p. 507.

26. *Ibid.*, p. 503.

27. *Ibid.*, p 14.

28. St. Louis edition, XVII, 2013 ff.

29. *Ibid.*, p. 102.

30. *Johannesburg Star*, September 25, 1967, p. 11.

31. Malcolm Muggeridge, "The Great Liberal Death-Wish," *National Review*, Vol. XVIII, No. 24 (June 14, 1966), p. 574.

32. Department of Theology, L. W. F. *Report* 1957-1963 (Helsinki Assembly, 1963, Document No. 7), pp. 17-18.

33. Bernard Ramm, *The Pattern of Authority* (Grand Rapids: Eerdmans, 1957), p. 51, quoted in: J. I. Packer, "*Fundamentalism and the Word of God*" (Grand Rapids: Eerdmans, 1958), p. 93, note 1.

34. Martin Luther , "To the Christian Nobility of the German Nation," Saemmtliche Schriften (St. Louis edition), X , 336.

35. *Ibid.*, p. 337.

36. Henry Bettenson, ed., *Documents of the Christian Church* (London: Oxford University Press, 1963), p. 282.

37. Bengt Haegglund, *Die Heiliges Schrift Und Ihre Deutung in der Theologie Johann Gerhard* (Lund: CWK Gleerup, 1951), passim.

38. J. I. Packer, OP. CIT., p. 34.

39. N. Nagel, "Anglican Christology of the Upper Stream From *Lux Mundi To Essays Catholic and Critical,*" Concordia Theological Monthly, Vol. XXVI, No. 6 (June, 1955), p. 419, note 45.

40. St. Louis edition, XX, 902-903.

41. Adolf Hoenecke, *Ev-Luth. Dogmatik* (Milwaukee Northwestern, 1909), Vol. I, p. 13.

42. *Ibid.*, pp. 13-14.

43. *Ibid.*, p. 40.

44. Malcolm Muggeridge, "The Dying Call of the Church of England," *The Bulletin* (Sydney), Vol. 38, No. 4435 (February 19, 1966), pp. 32 ff.

45. *Lehre Und Wehre*, January, 1879, p. 1.

Christian News, June 15, June 22, and June 29, 1970

1. Theology is and must be ____.
2. What has now the last word? ____
3. ____ reigns supreme.
4. "Scientific" theology is a program for ___ the truth rather than one for ____ the truth.
5. Luther said that doctrine must be absolutely ____.
6. Luther's doctrinal certainty is the very thing detested by ____.
7. What has happened to dogmatics today? ____
8. Dogmatics and exegesis are simply different ____.
9. Luther equates doctrine with ____.
10. Nicaea accepted the creed because ____.
11. Does the Church and her theologians have the authority to establish doctrines? ____
12. A doctrinal stand without binding force is ____.
13. The "Thirteen Theses" settled the ____.
14. The entire Formula of Concord was directed against ____.
15. Have new controversies in the church risen in the last 400 years?____
16. The time seems right for ____.
17. What is the "Collier's faith" Luther mentioned? ____
18. What is needed for our time as new heresies arise? ____
19. What did Joseph Sittler teach about Christ? ____
20. Deny the law of non-contradiction then every statement means the same as its ____.
21. Who is accused of rationalism" ____
22. An unhelpfully naive "Exegetical" approach is content to be allowed to pray with ____.
23. Christ teaches us to regard Scripture with ____.
24. What is a paradox? ____
25. The essentials of logic are ____.

26. Did Luther reject "Aristotelianism logic?" ____
27. Historical theology must be ____.
28. Divine truth was given not for speculation but ____.
29. What could happen in a hospital without standards? ____
30. In much of what passes for the church today a bureaucrat's right to be a bureaucrat takes ____.
31. What is infinitely more precious than biological life?____
32. What did Walther say about "the peaceable sitting together in pastoral conferences?" ____
33. True Christian theologians should have contempt for ____.
34. True theology must be realized in ____.

THE FACTUAL BASIS OF CHRISTIANITY

Review by Kurt Marquart
Reprinted from *LOGOS*

When Monica, the mother of the great St. Augustine of Hippo, begged an elderly bishop to talk to her brilliant boy about his Manichaean heresy, the bishop wisely refused. Having been a Manichee himself, he pointed out that young Augustine was puffed up with his new-found-knowledge. Debate would only entrench him more deeply in his cult. But the bishop was confident that, being a very intelligent young man, Augustine would sooner or later think his own way through and out of the pretentious tissue of fashionable nonsense that was Manicheeism. And so it happened. Afterwards Manicheeism had no more effective opponent than Augustine. He knew how to explode the system from within.

Professor John Warwick Montgomery, a young U.S. Lutheran theologian, is that same sort of man. He is not merely young, but representative of a "New-Breed." For him agnosticism was the starting point of his intellectual-spiritual Odyssey, and Christianity the point of arrival. This gives him a significant advantage over those who, having started in orthodoxy, are still reacting, often overreacting, against their upbringing, and are tending to see more merit in certain contemporary mind-sets than they actually have. (Christian student publications particularly tend to nurse that sort of intellectual inferiority complex by means of tedious self-flagellation).

Montgomery has, as it were, outgrown the fashionable secular superstitions. Their sacred cows are not objects of deference for him. In fact he quite enjoys tweaking their tails on occasion. He therefore has no apologies to make for his clear-headed commitment to Christianity as defined by its own documentary sources. And while others do their best to hide the intellectual consequences of such a position in a fog of unctuous evasions, Montgomery welcomes logical clarity and consistency, and indeed pursues them with rare analytical vigor. This alone should make Montgomery's work interesting to university students concerned about ultimate issues.

In future numbers we shall have occasion to review some of Montgomery's full-length books. The present 19 pp. booklet is a reprint of four short essays originally published in the I.V.F.'s HIS magazine.

The fundamental proposition against which Montgomery directed these four essays was the closing sentence from a lecture by a Professor Stroll on the subject, "Did Jesus Really Exist?":

> "An accretion of legends grew up about this figure (Jesus), was incorporated into the Gospels by various devotees of the movement, was rapidly spread throughout the Mediterranean world by the ministry of St. Paul; and that (sic) because this is so, it is impossible to separate these legendary elements in the purported descriptions of Jesus from those which in fact were true of him."

Now, one way of dealing with this type of approach is to evade it, with an air of profundity, thus: "Ah yes, but all this deals only with the shallow, hum-drum pedestrian level of mere historical facts! Faith leaps to the deep realities beyond and behind external facts!"

Montgomery is too clear-headed and well-informed to resort to this sort of cheap apologetics. He is convinced that historical facts do matter, particularly to believers in the incarnation, and that the factual evidence can be shown to substantiate the historical claims of the Christian religion. Indeed, he writes of himself: "Like Cambridge professor C. S. Lewis, I was brought 'kicking and struggling' into the kingdom of God by the historical evidence in behalf of Jesus' claims."

In the course of his expert demolition of Stroll's fallacies, Prof. Montgomery outlines the main features of this historical evidence. The argument is studded with little gems of relevant quotations from competent authorities. For example, this is what Sir Frederic G. Kenyon, formerly director and principal librarian of the British Museum, had to say about the textual advantage of the New Testament documents over all other ancient manuscripts:

"In no other case is the interval of time between the composition of the book and the date of the earliest extant manuscripts so short as in that of the New Testament. The books of the New Testament were written in the latter part of the first century; the earliest extant manuscripts (trifling scraps excepted) are of the fourth century—say, from 250 to 300 years later. This may sound a considerable interval, but it is nothing to that which parts most of the great classical authors from their earliest manuscripts. We believe that we have in all essentials on accurate text of the seven extant plays of Sophocles; yet the earliest substantial manuscript upon which it is based was written more than 1400 years after the poet's death. Aeschylus, Aristophanes, and Thucydides are in the same state; while with Euripides the Interval is increased to 1600 years. For Plato it may be put at 1300 years, for Demosthenes as low as 1200." (F. G . Kenyon, HANDBOOK TO THE TEXTUAL CRITICISM OF THE NEW TESTAMENT (2nd ed.; London: Macmillan,1912) page 5.)

That was written in 1912. Since then numerous papyri containing portions of the New Testament have been discovered. Evaluating this new evidence shortly before his death, Kenyon wrote, in 1940:

"The interval, then, between the dates of original composition and the earliest extant evidence becomes so small as to be in fact negligible, and the last foundation for any doubt that the Scriptures have come down to us substantially as they were written has now been removed. Both the AUTHENTICITY and the GENERAL INTEGRITY of the books of the New Testament may be regarded as finally established" (THE BIBLE AND ARCHEOLOGY (New York and London: Harper, 1940), pp. 199ff. Emphasis in original.

W. F. Albright, the world's foremost authority on Biblical archeology, has stated, with regard to the dating of the New Testament documents:

"In my opinion, every book of the New Testament was written by a baptized Jew between the forties and the eighties of the first century A.D. (very probably sometime between about 50 and 75 A.D.)" (Quoted in an interview for CHRISTIANITY TODAY, January 18, 1963).

This early dating of the New Testament writings, incidentally cuts the ground from under the "form-critical" approach, which assumes a development of the Christian tradition during a stage of oral transmission. Since the time span between the events and the written records is so short, there are no grounds for assuming that the latter distorted the former, particularly since eye-witnesses of the events, both sympathetic and hostile, were still available at the time of writing.

C. S. Lewis is quoted on Hume's argument against miracles:

"Now of course we must agree Hume that if there is absolutely 'uniform experience' against miracles, if in other words they have never happened, why then they never have. Unfortunately, we know the experience against them to be uniform only if we know that all the reports of them are false. And we can know all the reports to be false only if we know already that miracles have never occurred. In fact, we are arguing in a circle." (MIRACLES (New York: Macmillan, 1947). pp. 121-124).

While still an atheist, C.S. Lewis was shocked into an awareness of the strength of the Christian case:

"Early in 1926 the hardest boiled of all the atheists I ever knew sat in my room on the other side of the fire and remarked that the evidence for the historicity of the Gospels was really surprisingly good. 'Rum thing,' he went on. 'All that stuff of Frazer's about the Dying God. Rum thing. It almost looks as if it had really happened once.' To understand the shattering impact of it, you would need to know the man (who has certainly never since shown any interest in Christianity). If he, the cynic of cynics, the toughest of the toughs, were not—as I would still have put it— 'safe,' where could I turn? Was there then no escape?" (SURPRISED BY JOY (New York: Harcourt, Brace,1956), pp. 223-24.)

And here is an interesting little excursion into psychiatry by a practitioner of that art. Dr. J . T. Fisher:

"If you were to take the sum total of all authoritative articles ever written by the most qualified of psychologists and psychiatrists on the subject of mental hygiene—if you were to combine them and refine them and cleave out the excess verbiage—if you were to take the whole of the meat and none of the parsley, and if you were to have unadulterated bits of pure scientific knowledge concisely expressed by the most capable of living poets, you would have an awkward and incomplete summation of the Sermon on the Mount. And it would suffer immeasurably through comparison. For nearly two thousand years the Christian world has been holding in its hands the complete answer to its restless and fruitless yearnings. Here ... rests the blueprint for successful human life with optimum mental

102

health and contentment" (J.T. Fisher and L. S. Hawley, A FEW BUTTONS MISSING (Philadelphia: J . B. Lippincott, 1951), p. 273).

So much for the popular, pseudo-psychiatric superstition that it is "unhealthy" to try to live by Christian ethics! The quotation also has implications for Potter's recent B.B.C.—A.B.C. play "Son of Man." Christ was there portrayed as an uncouth lunatic with delusions of grandeur. Naturally it must be admitted that anyone who thinks he is God but isn't, must be demented. But are lunatics capable of articulating "the blueprint for successful human life with optimum mental health?"

The "Son of Potter" Version of Christ is a travesty of history. Roman Catholic Archbishop Knox of Melbourne raised an interesting point in his protest, when he asked if the A.B.C. would allow a similar treatment of Mohammed. It seems unlikely, although the historical evidence in that case is really juicy.

Montgomery's treatise is full of other highly quotable tidbits. Let two final samples suffice:

Professor Stroll had argued that the New Testament picture of Christ had evolved from the prevailing "messianic fever," as exemplified, for instance, in the Essene "messiahs" of the Dead Sea scrolls. Replies Montgomery:

> "This entire argument demonstrates a baleful and inexcusable ignorance of the nature of Jewish messianic expectation at the time of Christ. Historically it can be proven beyond question that on every important point Jesus' conception of Himself as Messiah differed radically from the conceptions held by all parties among the Jews. Particularly it cannot be harmonized with the Essene 'Teacher of Righteousness' described in the scrolls from the Dead Sea."

We conclude, appropriately with a penetrating comment about the foundational fact of Christianity, the Resurrection:

> "The factual character of the resurrection provided the disciples with the final proof of the truth of Jesus' claim to deity, and it provides the historian with the only adequate explanation for the conquering power of Christianity after the death of its founder. False messiahs of the time fell into obscurity because they could not back up their claims.
>
> "For example, Theudas in 44 A.D. promised a crowd that he would divide the waters of the Jordan River, and in 52-54 A.D. an unnamed 'Egyptian' messiah gathered a crowd of 30,000 Jews and said that at his command the walls of Jerusalem would fall down. But both incidents ended in ignominious failure, accompanied by bloodshed at the hands of the Roman soldiery. Christianity, however, flourished as a result of Jesus' attested claim to conquer the powers of death."

It would be difficult to find a more compact, yet documented, statement of the historical case for Christianity, than this little booklet by Montgomery.

Christian News, August 31,1970

1. Manacheeism had no more effective opponent than ____.
2. What sort of man is John Warwick Montgomery? ____
3. What was the starting point of Montgomery's intellectual-spiritual odyssey? ____
4. Do historical facts matter? ____
5. What is the difference between the earliest extant texts of the New Testament and those of Sophocles, Aristophanes, Thucydides, Plato etc.? ____
6. The authenticity and general integrity of the New Testament books may be regarded as finally ____.
7. Christianity flourished as a result of ____.

THE DOUBLE-EDGE SWORD
OF GOD'S WORD

1. The military "sword"-metaphor at first sight suggests that the holy Word of God is predominantly Law.

Rienecker's 1974 SPRACHLICHER SCHLUESSEL suggests instead a priestly-sacrificial meaning at Heb. 4:12, i.e. "Schlachtmesser," slaughtering knife, cf. Gen. 22.6.10. That seems to fit the context.

2. Yet in contexts of defense against demonic attacks upon the Church, the "sword of the Spirit" (Eph. 6:17) must be essentially the truth of the Gospel.

Certainly the undoing of the Man of Sin by the "breath of the Lord Jesus' mouth" (II Thes. 2:8) is pure Gospel for the Church! The idea of something "preventing" (vv. 6, 7) the "mystery of lawlessness" from flaunting itself openly suggests Thomas Hobbes' dictum: "The papacy is naught but the Ghost of the deceased Roman Empire sitting crowned upon the grave thereof" (cf. the Scarlet Woman of the Seven Hills, Rev. 17). This anti-Christian power was effectively unveiled not by moralists like Erasmus, but by the pure biblical GOSPEL restored to the Church by God through Martin Luther in the Reformation.

3. Both Law and Gospel are part and parcel of the one written Word of God, the Holy Scriptures.

4. Holy Scripture has absolute authority in the church not because it is Law and/or Gospel, but because it is the written Word of God, and therefore without error (II Tim. 3:15-17).

Large Catechism: "My neighbor and I—in short, all men—many err and deceive, but God's Word cannot err (nec errare nec fallere protest)" (Baptism, Tappert, p. 444).

James Packer, in "Fundamentalism" and the Word of God, calls the denial of biblical inerrancy "a species of impenitence."

Luther: "I beg and really caution every pious Christian not to be offended by the simplicity of the language and stories. . .but fully realize that, however simple they may seem, these are the very words, works, judgments and deeds of the majesty, power, and wisdom of the most high God. . . Simple and lowly are the swaddling clothes, but dear is the treasure, Christ, Who lies in them" (Luther's Works, 35:236).

5. The status and authority of the Old Testament as written Word of God are clear from the teaching of Christ (St. Jn. 10:35) and His Apostles (II Pet. 1:20-21).

6. The status and authority of the New Testament Scriptures are, if anything, even greater ("a more sure word of prophecy," II Pet. 1:19), since they proceed from the very fullness of Pentecost, as the Lord Himself had promised (St. Jn. 14:16-31; 15:20.26.;27; 16:13-15; 17:14-24; 20:31). See I Cor. 2:12.13.16; 14:37; II Thess. 2:15; 3:14, etc. The later books of the NT cite the earlier ones as "Scripture": Cf. I Tim. 5:18 and St. Lk. 10:7, and II Pet. 3:15.16 re. St. Paul's letters.

7. Perhaps the most urgent need of world-wide Lutheranism today is

a global confessional settlement, analogous to the Formula of Concord, of the issue of biblical authority and related matters, to the definitive exclusion of the decay-products of the cultural revolution of the so-called Enlightenment, above all the historical-critical corruption of what passes for "theology" today.

E. Brunner: "The fundamental error, which equates the revelation with revealed doctrine begins with the Apologists but has its beginnings even in the Pastoral Epistles and with the Apostles Fathers (cf. Titus 2:10, and the emphasis on 'sound doctrine'). The expression in 2 Tim. 3:16, 'Every scripture inspired by God is also profitable for teaching,' which, wrongly translated, became the locus classicus for the doctrine of verbal inspiration, betrays the beginnings of this unfortunate identification" (Revelation and Reason [Philadelphia: Westminster Press, 1946], pp. 8-9).

H. Asmussen: "But this is in fact the picture of wide sectors of out Lutheran Church today: clergymen read aloud the Christmas story, which they consider a fairytale. They read aloud the Easter story, to which they find access only after several reinterpretations. At the grave, they witness to the resurrection of the dead, which they consider a myth" (Lutheran World, Vol. 13, no. 2 [1966], p. 186).

Thomas Sheehan of Loyola University wrote in The New York Review (14 June 1984) of a developing "liberal consensus" in Roman Catholic biblical scholarship to the effect that "Jesus of Nazareth did not assert any of the divine or messianic claims the Gospels attributed to him and that he died without believing he was Christ the Son of God."

H. & M. Keller: "[Historical criticism] makes a difference to the way one thinks of Jesus. Is he a mighty being of superhuman power, who can manipulate [sic] the elements as he wills, stilling the storm and the waves, conjuring [sic] fish into the fisherman's net, abolishing the force of gravity, and altering his own material substance so that at one moment he is a man who can be touched and can eat and drink, and at the next a spirit who can pass through closed doors? Or is he an ordinary man who did nothing like this at all, and never wanted to; a man whose enormous significance expressed itself not in any physical abnormality [sic] but merely in his behavior and in his destiny?" (Miracles in Dispute, Fortress Press, 1979 p. 177).

John Reumann argued in the LWF's Lutheran World Report, June 1980, in celebration of the 450th anniversary of the Augsburg Confession, that Article III of the AC must be given up, since the whole traditional Christology, from Nicaea and Chalcedon to AC III is unbiblical and untenable in light of modern historical-critical scholarship (see 1981 LC-MS Resolution 3-20).

Radical Feminism: "They pray to God the Father and Mother Goddess and sing nonsexist hymns. Then they gather around a small table with a bell, a candle, and a Bible. The worship leader reads passages from the Bible that oppress women and the group cries out in unison: 'Out, demons, out!' At the close of this ritual 'Exorcism of Patriarchal Texts' a woman proclaims, 'These texts and all oppressive texts have lost their power over our lives" (Grenz-Olson, Twentieth Century Theology, p. 225).

Elizabeth Achtemeier: "No religion in the world is so old as is this immanentist identification of God with creation. It forms the basis of every nonbiblical religion, except Islam;...Worshippers of the Mother Goddess ultimately worship the creation and themselves, rather than the Creator" (Ibid., p. 236).

Dan Brown's The Da Vinci Code uses "alternative Gospels" to titillate his readers with the notion of "a physical relationship between Jesus and Mary Magdalene" (TIME, 22 Dec. 2003, 9. 56) No wonder a Zen priest could joke: "Had I known the Gospel of Thomas, I wouldn't have had to become a Buddhist!" (Ibid.).

Lutheran Church of Australia: "We therefore find ourselves opposed to many assumptions of 'higher' criticism, assumptions which have increasingly shaped the methods and conclusions of biblical scholarship in the last two hundred years. Some of these assumptions are:

(a) That the biblical documents must be treated in principle like all other historical documents, without regard to their claim to inspiration and authority;

(b) That science, history, and other disciplines are valid and legitimate norms and standards by which the truthfulness and reliability of biblical statements can and must be judged;

(c) That the miraculous aspects of the witness of the biblical writers may be discounted as an element of primitive culture;

(d) That the Apostles' and even our Blessed Lord's own understanding and interpretation of particular texts may in principle be regarded as defective or questionable, and as subject to progressive correction by subsequent biblical scholarship.

Such assumptions as these constitute an attack not only on the apostolicity of the Church (Eph. 2:20), but on the very Lordship of Christ. For this reason we reject them unconditionally.

"This does not mean that we reject either reason or scholarship...But everyone who takes the Reformation's SOLA SCRIPTURA seriously must insist that the proper function of reason, and thus of scholarship, is in every respect UNDER and not OVER Scripture--as handmaid, and not as mistress" (1972 Report, p. 362).

8. Unlike the anti-creedal sects, inspired by Zwingli-Calvinist enthusiasm ("Schwaermerei", "fanaticism"), the Church of the Augsburg Confession means by "SOLA SCRIPTURAL" not an "open Bible" to be interpreted as anyone might like, but the real and true sense of Scripture, confessed in opposition to errors, denials, and distortions in any article of faith.

Karl Barth insisted that the Reformed churches know only "a timeless appeal to the open Bible and to the Spirit which from it speaks to our spirit." And: "Our fathers had good reason for leaving us NO Augsburg Confession, authentically interpreting the word of God, NO Formula of Concord, NO 'Symbolical Books' which might later, like the Lutheran, come to possess an odor of sanctity. They left us only CREEDS, more than one of which begin or end with a proviso which leaves them open to being improved upon in the future. The Reformed churches simply do not know the word dogma, in its rigid hierarchical sense" (The Word of God and the Word of Man, pp. 229-230).

Smalcald Articles: [Enthusiasm] "is a poison implanted and inoculated in man by the old dragon, and it is the source, strength, and power of all heresy, including that of the papacy and Mohammedanism" (Tappert, p. 313).

Chesterton: "Of all the false religions in the world, the worst is enthusiasm, the worship of the god within. For that Jones shall worship the god within turns out ultimately to mean that Jones shall worship Jones."

The same: "The trouble with mysticism is threefold: It begins with mist, it centers in I and it ends in schism."

Ronald Knox: "Fanaticism feels it know not what. Faith knows what it does not feel."

9. The Church of the Augsburg Confession defends the biblical evangel ON JUSTIFICATION (GRACE ALONE!) (cf. I Cor. 15:3.4) against Rome and ON THE MEANS OF GRACE (culminating in the Real Presence of the Lord's Body and Blood in His Supper, cf. I Cor. 11:23 ff.) against Geneva and all their offspring.

The "Lutheran" World Federation, by compromising with the Vatican on Justification (the "Augsburg Concession" of 1999), and with the Zwingli-Calvinists on the Real Presence (Leuenberg Concord, 1973 and "Reconciled Diversity," i.e. "genuine church fellowship" among the various confessions, yet "the legitimacy of the confessional differences and therefore the need to preserve them," 1977, Dar-es-Salaam) has shown itself to be the chief agency for the destruction of the Lutheran Confession in today's world.

10. The most important aspect of "rightly dividing [cutting straight] the Word of truth" (II Tim. 2:15) is to distinguish clearly between the letter that kills, and the Spirit that makes alive (II Cor. 3:6), i.e. LAW AND GOSPEL. This involves also the vital distinction between the Two Governments ("Kingdoms"), i.e. spiritual and temporal authority or rule.

"The distinction between law and Gospel is an especially brilliant light which serves the purpose that the Word of God may be rightly divided and the writings of the holy prophets and apostles may be explained and understood correctly." (Formula of Concord, S.D. V, 1 Tappert, p. 558).

Dean Edward Norman of Peterhouse, Cambridge, asks "what will happen to Christianity as its content is drained away into the great pool of secular idealism" in light of lunacies like the Spring, 1978, meeting of the British Council of Churches re. [Red] China: "The Reverend (Miss) Lee Ching Chee (of Hong Kong) contrasted the many Churches in Hong Kong with the lack of them in China: she asked whether the people of Hong Kong were any more Christian than those of China. The Reverend Dr. John Fleming underlined this when he asserted that God still lives in China today, not because there are Christians there, but because He is at work there, confronting us with what He is doing through non-Christians, through science, through political leaders" (Christianity and the World Order, B.B.C. Reith Lectures, 1978, pp. 12-13).

11. Out Good Physician, Who is Love Incarnate, does His "alien work" (diagnosis/Law) only for the sake of His "own, proper work" (cure/Gospel): "for I came not to judge the world, but to save the world" (St. John 12:47). Also St. Jn. 5:39: "You search the Scriptures, for in them you think you have eternal life; yet they testify of Me."

"The Cross alone is our theology--CRUX sola est nostra theologia," M. Luther, WA 5:176.

The "Full Gospel" is not Preaching plus "miracles" (see St. Mt. 13:39; I Cor. 1:22-24), but preaching plus Sacraments--exactly the Three Witnesses of I Jn. 5:78! whatever departs from the APOSTOLIC Gospel (Acts 2:42) is to that extent apostatic (Gal. 1:8.9).

12. The Three Witnesses on earth, the Spirit, the Water, and the Blood, are the real constituents of the true unity of the Church, as confessed in our evangelical, ecumenical Magna Charta, the Seventh Article of the Augsburg Confession:

It is sufficient for the true unity of the Christian church that the Gospel be preached there unanimously according to its pure (i.e. biblical) understanding, and that the sacraments be administered according to the divine word (German text).

Not necessary for the true unity of the church are outward human traditions, like church structure ("apostolic succession"), ceremonies, customs, etc. See Max Thurian, ed., Churches Respond to BEM (Baptism, Eucharist, Ministry, 1982 Lima Statement of the Faith and Order Commission, WCC), III: 49: "The subject of the ministry divides the churches more strongly than baptism and eucharist and consequently the ministry section of the text is longer and more discursive." And pp. 52-53: "(The Reformation), whatever its positive results, shattered the unity of the Church in the West and introduced the contrast between the traditional structure of the ministry and the structures which developed from the Reformation, which are among the principal ecumenical problems of today." Again: "This estimate of the threefold order as not prescribed by Holy Scripture and yet desirable for unity is a position members of the Church of England will welcome" (p. 53, Church of England's Response).

13. In a world hypnotized by weapons of mass destruction, God the Most Blessed Trinity, in His three earthly witnesses, the Spirit, the Water, and the Blood (I Jn. 5:7-8, cf. St. Jn. 6: 63: "My words, they are spirit and they are life"), equips and supplies His holy Church and Mission in superabundance with the weapons of mass salvation!

Metango, Kenya, February 17, 2004
Christian News, May 3, 2004

1. Sword of the Spirit must be essentially ____.
2. Holy Scripture has absolute authority in the church because it is the ___.
3. The later books of the New Testament cite the earlier ones as ____.
4. Perhaps the most urgent need for world Lutheranism today is ____.
5. John Reumann argued in the LWF Report that the whole traditional

Christology is ____.

6. Reason is ____ Scripture and not ____ Scripture.
7. Barth insisted that the Reformed simply do not know the word ____.
8. The Church of the Augsburg Confession defends the biblical evangelism on ____.
9. The Lutheran World Federation has shown itself to be the chief agency of the ____ of the Lutheran Confessions in today's world.
10. What is the Augsburg Concession of 1999? ____.
11. The "Full Gospel" is not preaching plus miracles but preaching plus ____.
12. What equips and supplies His holy Church with the weapons of mass salvation? ____

"CHURCH GROWTH" AS MISSION PARADIGM—A LUTHERAN ASSESSMENT

"After all the bravado about CGM'S (Church Growth Movement) 'scientific' methods, it is startling to read C. Peter Wagner's recent conclusion: 'I don't think there's anything intrinsically wrong with the church growth principles we've developed, or the evangelistic techniques we're using. Yet somehow they don't seem to work.' (Christianity Today, June, 1991) Writes Professor Kurt Marquart in the recently published "'Church Growth' as Mission Paradigm—A Lutheran Assessment." The 153-page book's cover illustration appears to the right.

C. Peter Wagner is a leading spokesman for the Church Growth Movement. In more recent years he has also become a prominent charismatic who claims to have the power to heal, including the ability to lengthen legs. Lutherans involved in the Church Growth Movement have been ardent supporters of Wagner and other Reformed and charismatic Church Growth leaders. Wagner wrote the preface of a book by Dr. Waldo Werning, a Lutheran Church- Missouri Synod Church Growth leader.

Marquart takes issue with some of the views expressed by Werning, David Luecke, Kent Hunter, James Dretke, Robert Scuderi, Oscar Feucht, and other LCMS supporters of the Church Growth Movement. Hunter, President of Church Growth Center, Corunna, Indiana, was one of the main speakers at a "Created to Praise" conference held last month at St. John's Lutheran Church, Ellisville, Missouri. The conference was sponsored by Dave and Barb Anderson's The Fellowship Ministries, Tempe, Arizona. A brochure listing the speakers and topics is reproduced on p. 12 of this issue of Christian News. Marquart, a professor at the Lutheran Church-Missouri Synod's Concordia Seminary, Ft. Wayne, Indiana, writes:

CHURCH GROWTH DOES NOT WORK

God's Redemption of the World

"The first focus, represented by the vertical funnel, is on God's redemption of the world in His Son. This is so basic that Christians of all Trinitarian confessions affirm it in principle. One simply cannot be a Christian and deny that the decisive events for human salvation have occurred in the life, death, and resurrection of Jesus Christ (St. John 1:1-18; 3:16; 6:48-51; 14:6; Acts 4:12; Rom. 5:15-19; 1 Cor. 15; II Cor. 5:19-21; 1 John 5:11,12). Even modern Roman Catholic theologians who hold, in the wake of the universalism of Vatican II, that salvation is effectively available and distributed also in Hinduism, Buddhism, and other pagan religions, nonetheless maintain that only Jesus Christ, and not Buddha or Mohammed or anyone else, actually obtained this salvation for mankind by His redemptive work.

"Yet despite the surface appearance of a broad inter-confessional consensus, there are far-reaching disagreements among the Lutheran,

111

Roman Catholic, and Reformed paradigms already about the crucial first focus. The Roman Catholic Council of Trent strongly condemns the doctrine of free justification and salvation by grace through faith in Christ alone. This implies that Christ did not earn for us the gift of salvation, but rather only the opportunity to earn salvation with His help. In technical terms, this denies the *intensive perfection* of Our Lord's redemptive work. Strict Calvinism, on the other hand, denies the *extensive perfection* of Christ's work, by teaching that He died not for all, but only for those predestined by God to eternal life. Another way of saying this is that Arminians among the Reformed—deny *grace alone*, while Geneva denies *universal grace*. There are easily accessible discussions of these matters in F. Pieper's *Christian Dogmatics*. Only the Wittenberg Reformation, with its teaching of full and free forgiveness and salvation obtained for all mankind by Christ— 'Objective Justification,' although that term came later—confesses full-strength both *grace alone* and *universal grace*. These differences are foundational, and work themselves out further 'downstream' along the whole line of Christian doctrine" (9-10).

The Pure Preaching of the Gospel

"If there is to be such a thing as Lutheran 'paradigm' for the church's mission, its all-decisive, determining elements will have to be the pure preaching of the Gospel (orthodoxy!) and the right administration of the sacraments (infant baptism, bodily presence!)—and therefore also properly qualified incumbents of the divinely ordained Gospel ministry to do this. All stress is on God's gracious channels of salvation, on His own provisions for the delivery of His deliverance in His Son—to the exclusion of all man-made substitutes, like synergism, moralism, unionism, antinomianism, revivalism, anti-sacramentalism, subjectivism, millenialism, Pentecostalism, and the like. Administrative, ceremonial, and other such details are significant only as they either implement and express, or else hinder and obstruct, the divine arrangements for the life and growth of the church (Augsburg Confession VII, compare Formula of Concord X)" (13).

Werning and Religious Quackery

"There are two shallow fallacies which should be eliminated at once. One is that 'Church Growth' is so nebulous that it can be whatever anybody wishes it to be. This impression is perhaps linked to a second fallacy, to the effect that the Church Growth Movement (CGM for short) is only about methods, and has little if any theological substance" (14).

"Waldo Werning (1992) states: 'Methodology and theology must be separated. Church Growth methodology did not grow out of Armenian [sic] theology'(p. 188). 'Church Growth,' he holds, is as theology-neutral as preaching: 'We don't Lutheranize preaching any more than we Lutheranize Church Growth. As Lutherans and Reformed utilize preaching, so Lutherans and Reformed utilize Church Growth' (p. 201). Then in the next paragraph: 'Church Growth does not mean a set of sociological principles added to biblical faith. Biblical faith is the base for Church

Growth.' While pleading for fair judgment on Church Growth, Werning denounces Steve Scheiderer's fine STM thesis on the subject, approved by me, as 'academical bankruptcy' (p. 201), and as the start and basis of a 'war' (p. 192), waged by 'a few' Ft. Wayne '"doctrinal experts' ...practicing religious quackery"' (p. 202)" (p. 14).

The Fruit of Reformed Theology

"Robert Koester (1993) is quite right in arguing that Church Growth is a fruit of Reformed theology, and of its Arminian branch—by far the larger today—at that. Instead of relying on the means of grace, the CGM bedazzles susceptible clergy and churches (and especially bureaucrats!) with flowcharts, 'diagnostic' numbers-crunching, and scientific-sounding jargon. Mixed with the familiar mission-exhortations of popular Protestantism, this salvation-technology entices the pietist/pragmatist mindset with its promise of a down-to-earth, 'do-able' science of religious engineering, which, if only we get it right, will produce growth.

"The growth for which churches vaguely yearn, says McGavran, 'is theirs if they will only do the right things. The church, as it exists in community after community, is sitting on the edge of great growth, provided it will do the right things.' When Win Arn asked, 'What do you mean by right things?' McGavran replied: 'It's partly method. It's partly attitude. It's partly theological positions. It's partly prayer. But most of all, it is recognizing that God wants the church to grow...' (McGavran and Arn, 1974:12).

"Towns, Vaughan, and Seifert, having warmly commended Robert Schuller and other leaders of the '100 largest' churches, conclude their chapter on 'faith and goal-setting' with two telling examples. A 'Bible-Baptist' explains: 'When I speak of hard work, I refer to man's part. Of course, I realize that God must work and He does so through yielded, dedicated men, but there is no spiritual secret to building a fast-growing church.' Another, a famous Pentecostalist, stated that the Holy Spirit 'had spoken to him and told him' to raise one hundred thousand dollars for a theological school library. He then 'applied highly motivational techniques' to realize the 'Spirit-given vision' (1982:210)" (p. 22-23).

"Lutheran" Church Growth?

"In view of all this it is startling to read in Kent Hunter (1983:27): 'A church growth philosophy of ministry is built on the means of grace (Word and Sacraments) and on prayer.' As a Lutheran, Hunter is clearly obliged to make the means of grace central and crucial. He is not entitled, however, to make believe that 'Church Growth' itself is 'built on' the means of grace. It clearly is built on nothing of the sort. That should have been evident already from what Hunter himself had said earlier in the same book: 'Church growth principles are beginning to spring up throughout major Protestant denominations as they turn their attention toward health and growth' (pp. 13-14). What do 'major Protestant denominations' know about means of grace? Hunter also holds that 'church growth teaching causes a church to come alive' (p. 17). So which is it then,

113

church growth teaching or the means of grace? They are not the same.

"Hunter's verbal tributes to the means of grace have a hollow ring. In *Global Church Growth*, 'the chief publication of the Church Growth Movement,' which he edits, Hunter printed an interview With Pastor Kim of the Yoido Full Gospel (Pentecostal) Church in Seoul, Korea. This is what we are told there about the meaning and benefit of church-attendance.

> When we repent of our sins, we can run to the church on Sunday morning because our hearts and our consciences are clean. Prayer makes people repent of their sins, and that makes people go running to their churches. Every Sunday we see many Christians running to Yoido Full Gospel Church. We emphasize that people should pray an hour every day. We urge them to come to church on Friday night. So they pray, and they repent of their sins, and their hearts are cleansed. This empowers them to come to the Lord and the church every Sunday morning.

"This was followed by an account of the Holy Spirit directing Dr. Cho, while praying, to move his church to Yoido Island. In sum:

> When we pray, the Holy Spirit speaks to our hearts. We obey the word of the Holy Spirit. So prayer is very important. Through prayer we can repent of our sins, and through prayer we can hear the still, small voice of our Lord. Through prayer, people's hearts are cleansed, and they go running to their church without any guilt.

"Hunter offers no correctives here about the means of grace, but refers to Pastor Kim as 'a great expert on the relationship between prayer and church growth,' and concludes with thanks and a hearty 'God bless your work!'

"What doesn't seem to register at all in this glorification of the 'largest church in the world,' is the vast chasm between a means-of-grace outlook and its opposite. In the biblical view, 'divine service' means first of all receiving forgiveness, life, and salvation from God. God serves us before we can serve Him (St. John 13:6-9). To receive His forgiveness in His Son 'is the highest way of worshiping Christ.' We run to church not to celebrate the 'clean conscience' or freedom from guilt which we already have in some other, independent way, but precisely to obtain and renew those gifts" (28, 29).

"At its Calvinistic best 'Church Growth' relies on the Reformed pietistic direct encounter with the Spirit in prayer. At its Arminian (synergistic) worst, it projects a manipulative religious engineering. Where everything depends on techniques and methods developed and certified as 'effective' by 'science.' Even the secular media see something tacky here: 'CGM experts judge a minister's accountability not by his faithfulness to the Gospel but whether, as Schaller puts it, "the people keep coming and giving"' (*Newsweek*, 17 December 1990, p. 52). The April 5, 1993 issue of *Time* quotes Methodist D. Stephen Long of Duke University's Divinity School as warning against 'patterning the church after a mega-supermarket.' While not objecting 'to the churches using some marketing techniques,' Long fears that 'what is happening is that marketing techniques are beginning to use the church.' The August 9, 1993 *Newsweek*, having noted that the mainline denominations may be dying from loss of theological integrity, comments: The only thing worse, perhaps, would be the rise of a new Protestant establishment that succeeds because it never had any'!" (p. 30).

LCMS Mission Director Scuderi and George

"What comes after 'megachurch'? 'Meta-church.' Church Growthist Carl F. George's book on the subject (1992) was described in an enthusiastic foreword by C. Peter Wagner as 'the most significant step forward in church-growth theory and practice. . . since 1970.' Some subheadings of Chapter Seven, 'Structure Cells to Do Pastoral Care,' tell the story: 'Laypeople Do the Pastoring . . . Pastoring Supersedes Teaching . . . Lay Pastors Look Beyond Dropouts and Failures . . .' The great example is again the Pentecostal Yoido Full Gospel Church in Seoul,* and the goal is constant multiplication of the basic unit, the 'cell' group. The leader of each nurturing group functions as a lay pastor to that 'ten-or-so person flock,' we are told (p. 98). Also: 'Cell leaders may be of either gender, even as the group may be single sex or mixed sexes.' Traditional terms like pastor, elder, and deacon are replaced with an annoying Roman numeral algebra of X's, L's, and D's, partly to avoid the awkward fact that 'certain texts' are taken to 'imply age- and gender-based qualifications' (pp. 129-135). Further: 'The teaching gift cannot be valued above the pastoring function'—done by lay men or women (p. 99).

"The 'deepest focus' of the name 'meta-church' is meant to be 'on change: Pastors' changing their minds about how ministry is to be done. . .' (p. 51). In his book, which has become a bible for some in the Missouri Synod's mission establishmen, George 'highlights the lay-led small group as the essential growth center,' so that 'everything else is to be considered secondary to its promotion and preservation' (p. 41)—for example, 'worship': (pp. 37, 38).

"The book has been distributed free of charge (at what cost to the Synod?) to pastors in some districts. Synodical World Missions Director Scuderi has produced a widely-distributed video, 'Church Extension Through Leadership Development,' 1992, which is basically a rehash of George's book" (37).

"The Lord's Supper is entirely beyond the scope of the book's interest. Baptism is trivialized like this: Following Luecke's (1988) 'village church/camp meeting' paradigm, George commends the 'camp meeting' way in which people 'must give a testimonial and tell the story of their religious experience,' in response to which 'the community extends tokens of acceptance (applause, friendship, membership, baptism, and so on), resulting in a sense of belonging for the newcomers' (p. 72)" (38).

Evangelism and Joel Heck

"Perfect sense though all this makes from a Pentecostal point of view, one can hardly imagine anything more diametrically opposed to the biblical, Lutheran preaching-and-sacraments orientation. Yet instead of warning against the book's deductions, much of our Synod's official 'missions' and 'evangelism' leadership zealously distributes it and advocates its 'meta-church' message! No more substantive correctives appear to be offered than a sprinkling of ritual incantations about 'Word and Sacrament'! There is no hint of an inkling of just how contrary this 'paradigm' is to our Confession's whole understanding of the Gospel. Indeed, Evangelism editor Joel Heck hails the volume in a fulsome review under the heading 'The Best Evangelism Book of the Decade.' Heck grants that people with certain prejudices won't like the book—for instance those who 'become easily upset when people apply the term pastor loosely to laypeople (in a nontechnical sense, not referring to the ordained clergy).' While the book is as flawed as any effort by flawed humans, Heck assures us, 'there is nothing inherently flawed about Meta-Church theory, for its approach to ministry is nothing less than a New Testament approach' (p. 12)" (39).

Radical Shift in Ministry Thinking

"It is surprising how naïve even Lutherans are about the toxic bite of this Church Growth bug. Kent Hunter, for instance, who holds that 'Church growth is a philosophy of ministry':

> The pastor is the called shepherd of the royal priesthood, but he is not there to do ministry for the sheep. Shepherds don't reproduce sheep, anyway. Sheep reproduce sheep!

> Mission and ministry lifelong to the people. The pastor is there to be the trainer, the equipper of the people . . . He does ministry himself, but his primary responsibility is to train Christians to do this ministry.

> ...Jesus was a model for His disciples...The pastor is to be a model for the members. He shows them how... He is to demonstrate how to counsel and witness. He is a model for ministry (1983:65).

"No! The Lord said not, 'Organize My sheep into work-brigades, to do the real ministry themselves,' but, 'Feed My lambs. Feed My sheep!' The shepherds are there precisely to 'do ministry for the sheep,' that is to preach the Gospel and administer the sacraments to them. The church is not a self-service buffet" (p. 42, 43).

'The Reformation confessed the New Testament teaching that everyone is a *priest* but not everyone a *minister*. This great truth is garbled by the Church Growth Movement into the modern populist falsehood that 'everyone is a minister'" (p. 46).

Novelty "Gifts"

"Church Growth founder Donald McGavran held that 'twenty-four separate gifts, all given by the Holy Spirit are mentioned in the New Testament,' that additional gifts not mentioned there might be available today, and that these various gifts 'are essential for church growth' (McGavran and Arn, 1973:35). C. Peter Wagner treats of 27 gifts, but is 'open-ended' about this number (1979:57 ff.)" (49).

"In a later book Wagner identified himself with the 'Third Wave of the Holy Spirit,' which followed in the 1980's upon the first and second waves of Pentecostalism and the 'charismatic movement' respectively (Wagner, 1988a). See also Wagner's 'Third Wave' article in the *Dictionary of Pentecostal and Charismatic Movements* (1988b).

"According to 'Lutheran charismatics' one finds in the movement 'a move conscious expectation and experience of the entire range of spiritual gifts that we find in Scripture, which, moreover, 'are seen as indispensable for the building up of the body of Christ, the church' (L. Christenson, 1987: 32)"(50).

"Later Wagner argues that people must carry out the 'roles' even if they lack the 'gifts' (pp. 90 ff.), and that 'not everyone who has the office of pastor needs the gift of pastor, and furthermore there are many men and women with the gift of pastor who do not have the office of pastor by being placed on a church staff' (p. 144). Preaching is not listed as a special 'gift,' and would be no more useful than 'making movies' or 'radio broadcasting' (ibid.). Robert Schuller, we are told, 'like most other super-church pastors, does not have the gift of pastor' [layministers attend to that] (p. 152). But he has something much better: The gift of faith—that is, the vision that produced the 'Crystal Cathedral' in Garden Grove, California** (p. 159). Others with that gift are 'Ralph Winter and Bill Bright and Oral Roberts and Cameron Townsend and Cho Yonggi who have given public demonstration of their gift of faith often measured by multi-million dollar projects' (p. 161). Fantasy has largely replaced the New Testament here" (52).

Pentecostal "Specials"

"With the apostles (St. Paul!) and prophets, the church at Corinth had all the fullness of Christ, signaled by such special manifestations (*phaneroosis*, 1 Cor. 12:7) of His Spirit as He had chosen to give. Also today of course God's hand is not shortened (Is. 59:1). He can and does in His wise and gracious providence act miraculously when and where He pleases, especially in answer to His people's prayers. But that special aura of 'signs' which accompanied the apostolic prophetic foundation of the church—and which Satan seeks to counterfeit, II Thess. 2:9—is to be expected today no more than are new apostles and prophets (see also the implications of Heb. 1:1-4; 2:1-4). Nor can such things be 'restored' or organized into a movement of 'renewal,' as also Missouri Synod 'charismatics' fancy. Rather, what is permanent, for all time, is the witness of the 'spirit, the water, and the blood' (1 Jn. 5:6-8). Whoever has Christ in His means of grace is 'complete in Him' (Col. 2:9). The 'full Gospel' is not 'preaching plus miracles' (the Pentecostal dream), or 'preaching plus "gifts"' (the charismatic/Church Growth fantasy), but *preaching plus sacraments*. The preaching-and-sacraments office established by Christ in the extraordinary form of His Apostolate, continues today in the ordinary Gospel ministry, I Cor. 4:1 ('the preaching office derives from the common call of the apostles,' *Treatise of the Power and Primacy of the*

Pope, 10, German, my translation). It is this divinely established Gospel-preaching office that Pentecostal Church Growthism is determined to be rid of: 'Until we count "ordination" of Sunday School teachers and distributors of church flowers as no different in essence from "ordination" of an elder or bishop, we cannot claim to be functioning as the body of Christ" (55, 56).

"L. Christenson's *Welcome, Holy Spirit*, regularly recommended in 'Renewal In Missouri's' *RIM Report*,*** states: 'If the charismatic renewal gives particular attention to spiritual gifts, it is because we believe that the restoration of the full spectrum of spiritual gifts to the church is part of the Lord's present strategy (p. 25). Also: The charismatic renewal has arisen in response to a sovereign move of the Spirit of God in the latter half of the 20th century' (p. 23)" (56).

His Love Our Response

"Presumably Lutherans believe in means of grace, and so would balk at the whole idea of a 'gift of evangelist' in the Wagner sense. Instead, it has been welcomed together with the rest of 'the gifts,' not only by Hunter (1985a:64), Werning (1977:38), and *Evangelism*, but by official Missouri Synod entities as well. The 1985 *His Love—Our Response* series, evidently adapted by the synodical Stewardship Department from the Texas District *Personal Renewal Study*, defined as follows: 'an evangelist shares the Gospel verbally with the unbeliever in such a way that he/she becomes a disciple of Christ.' Unlike the Texas prototype, the synodical version at least treated the Eph. 4:11 list under the rubric of the office of public ministry.' Other-wise it caved in helplessly to C. Peter Wagner's alien systematic theology about 'gifts.' Of the 'special gift' of 'tongues' we read: 'It is *not* in accord with Scripture to suggest that this gift ceased with the New Testament era.' And although 'some Christians feel that the office of the apostle no longer exists today,' the Teachers Manual maintained: 'An apostle exercises general leadership and direction in the church-at-large. A District official could serve in this capacity' (p. 13)! Although the means of grace are mentioned, the overall impression is that 'the gifts' are, as it were, enzymes, which activate and enable the Word and Sacraments to do any real good. That's what happens when one tries to 'Lutheranize' a neo-Pentecostal paradigm of church and mission. Our supine gullibility in the face of this 'gifts' cult is a sad measure of our theological impoverishment. The Southern Baptists, incidentally, 'have a table game for discovering gifts called "Nexus"' (Wagner, 1979:255)" (58-60).

"According to an official report, *Church Growth Survey Results in 1987*, sent to all synodical districts and seminaries by the Steering Committee of N.A.M.E, (North American Mission Executives), '22 Districts went through a multi-year process,' which involved about 900 congregations. 'Most of these 22 Districts, plus 12 others, used many "outside" consultants (Win and Chip Arn, Kent Hunter, Elmer Matthias, Lyle Schaller, Steve Wagner, and Waldo Werning most frequently) for a wide range of workshops.' This resulted in 'taking on "church growth eyes," that prompted changes in programs...In order of frequency, the resulting changes were evident in more churches planted, more creative emphasis on witnessing, spiritual gift programs, discerning community and congregational needs, increased Bible Study, and a growing confidence among leaders'" (58). "Hunter, Werning, and His Love—Our response all repeat Wagner's five steps for discovering one's gift(s): Explore the possibilities, experiment with as many as you can, examine your feelings, evaluate your effectiveness, expect confirmation from the Body (1979: 116-133)"(59).

Unbiblical Systematics

"A dear warning signal that one has forsaken Scripture for a false systematics, is the doctrinaire claim that 'gifts of the Spirit' are one thing (properly called 'charismata'), and 'fruit of the Spirit' (Gal. 5:22.23) quite another. Hunter (1985a: 180), Werning (1977:38), and *His Love—Our Response* (Teachers Manual, p. 7), all follow Wagner on this point (1979:88). While admitting that 'in a sense the fruit of the Spirit is a gift,' *His Love—Our Response* adds at once: 'But the fruit is not a charisma.' But why not? This pet notion that 'charisma' is a technical term for 'gifts' but not 'fruit' of the Spirit is baseless" (60).

Need for Compelling Sense of Church

"With these considerations we have already entered upon the subject of worship in the specific sense of what happens in church. Those who are always urging new 'paradigms,' are quite right about one thing: Church attendance can no longer be taken for granted. In the 'good old days' going to church was often simply the done thing. Its value was woven into the social, ethnic fabric, and so was part and parcel of what bound communities together. All this has changed completely since the 'cultural revolution' made secularism the established religion. For most of our contemporaries it is by no means self-evident that going to church matters very much. As a shrewd observer put it to me some years ago: 'Christians going to church remind me of an army that's forever saluting and parading, but never carrying out orders!' Church services then are ceremonial tinsel, not the real stuff of religion. What we need more than ever before is a truly compelling vision of the importance of 'church,' and that cannot be created from opinion surveys among outsiders. It must arise from the deepest nature of Christian faith itself. Only a church which doesn't give a rap about what Hollywood or 'Baby Boomers' or the Supreme Court think, can be taken seriously by anyone with any respect for religion—never mind Christianity!" (80-81).

The Lutheran World Federation and LBW

"More's the pity therefore that modern Lutherans by and large have frittered away this heritage. The 'Lutheran' World Federation, for instance, urges altar and pulpit fellowship with the Calvinist/Zwinglian churches, and thus the abandonment of the Sacrament of the Altar as confessed in the Book of Concord. In America, the Lutheran Book of Worship (1978) was deeply influenced by the Four Actions scheme of Gregory Dix (1945). According to this view the constitutive elements of the Holy Supper are the offertory procession, the Eucharistic prayer, the breaking of the bread, and the distribution. The Words of Institution are absorbed into the eucharistic prayer, as in the pre-Reformation canon. Contrast these ritual formalities with our evangelical confession of the three-fold God-given action: Consecration (Words of Institution), distribution, and reception (*Formula of Concord*, SD VII, 86). *"He Is Risen—And He Is Here!*

"What's the difference? Well, the Four Actions view again turns the Sacrament basically into something which we offer to God. Of course there's nothing wrong with sacrifices of praise and thanksgiving in response to the Divine Gifts (see Apology XXIV, 74). But the essence of the Sacrament is God's giving and doing, and that remains primary. Our responses are not the Sacrament, and remain secondary. The Four Actions scheme ignores this difference, and turns God's Self-giving into the church's self-offering to God, the Sacrament back into a sacrifice. The result of such thinking is that the actual Sacramental Presence of the Lord's Body and Blood fades into relative unimportance, and with it the consecratory power of the Words of Institution as that to which the Lord 'has attached his own command and deed' (*Formula of Concord*, SD VII, 78)" (88, 89).

Entertainment Evangelism

"In the face of the lunacies now masquerading as worship, one can only admire the wit of the woman who thought it was high time for the church 'to stop trying to entertain the goats and get back to feeding the sheep' (p. 72). It was, one must remember, the devil who invented 'entertainment evangelism,' and tempted the Lord with it (St. Mt. 4:5.6)" (100).

Frantic Cries for Change For Missionary Health

"Reading that in 1957, who would have predicted the devastations to come? Meanwhile the fairly conservative American Lutheran Church was first stampeded into church-fellowship with the Reformed, and then disappeared into an ELCA which stands for everything and nothing, including the surrender of the Sacrament, on the altar of ecumenism. There can be no doubt that sloppiness about practice— 'mere adiaphora'!—was a softening-up for deeper disaster. And now the same dynamic is upon the Missouri Synod, in the frantic cries for change for the sake of the missionary health and growth of the church" (106).

"We may begin by noting that 'culture' has become something of a fetish in missionary discourse. The odd thing is that for all its 'scientific' airs. Church Growth is open to the criticism that it is wedded to an antiquated anthropology (functionalism) with faulty notions of culture" (107).

Real Racism

"What really is racist, surely, is a missiological approach which implies that African-Americans are genetically predestined to be Baptists or Pentecostalists! That is akin to the patronizing attitude which would deprive non-western churches of traditional hymnody. Taber (1991:140) reports a friend in Ghana once having told him: 'I feel no need to return to traditional Fanti music; I like *Hymns Ancient and Modern*. I'm not ready to "return" to the music of my ancestors that I don't know'" (110).

Hymnals

"The governing principle must be that expressed in the title of my colleague Richard Resch's splendid essay, 'Hymnody as Teacher of the Faith' (1993b). Since hymns shape our minds and souls, it is important that they contain the church's faith, and not falsehood or drivel like 'I'm gonna walk, wa wa sing la la' (Resch, 1993a:25). It is alarming therefore that many of our parishes do not use the church's hymn-books at all (their use is even officially discouraged in some Church Growthist districts), but use unchurchly materials like *The Other Song Book* (Resch, 1993b:164)"(111).

"However, one must beware of an overdone purism here. No matter how good the sixteenth century chorales, for instance, a steady diet of only those narrows the range unduly. Who would want to do without St. Patrick's 'I bind unto myself today, Thy strong Name of the Trinity,' or R. V. Williams' 'For all the saints'? But even traditional English hymns like 'Holy, holy, holy,' or 'The Church's one Foundation' should not be despised merely because they are, or were, popular. The hymns of St. Ambrose of Milan were enormously popular at the time, as were of course those of Martin Luther twelve hundred years later. So winsome was the antiphonal chanting in Milan that some of the Arian soldiers who had been sent to surround and intimidate Ambrose's church, laid down their weapons and joined the congregational singing.

"It is pedantic to hold that the only 'good Lutheran' hymns are hymns written by Lutherans during or since the Reformation! Hymns which have become a part of the Christian consciousness of English-speaking people everywhere, may not—unless they are outright badges of falsehood—be neglected by English-speaking Lutherans. They are 'sanctified by the Word of God and prayer' (1 Tim. 4:5), in the liturgy. Simple hymns like 'Just as I am' or 'Rock of Ages' acquire deep sacramental significance when sung during the Distribution, a meaning that is frustrated by the smoke and mirrors of revivalism. The most popular hymn in the English language today is said to be 'Amazing Grace.' That should not be held against it, although care should be taken to have it sung in a churchly, not a sentimental way. The same goes for 'Go Tell It On the Mountain.' All the hymns mentioned are included in Lutheran Worship, along with some less happy choices. There is no need therefore to depart from the 'exclusive use of doctrinally pure agenda, hymnbooks, and catechisms in church and school,' laid down in the Synodical Constitution (VI,4) among the 'Conditions of Membership.' Especially in our age of the photocopier, the occasional use of an acceptable hymn from other sources for special occasions falls of course well within the intent of this very necessary rule.

"The church, it must be remembered, is not a museum for the preservation of obscure cultural treasures, the more obscure the better. She is the living Body of Christ, and takes pleasure in glorifying Him from whom all blessings flow" (111-113).

"I Believed, Therefore Have I Spoken"

"Why is it then that we Lutherans with our pure Gospel and sacraments have not been firebrands of missionary dynamism? Is it because our faith is drab and old-fashioned, and we haven't managed to spiff it up for modern tastes? Or is it because we have not been trained in the right ways of saying it? Or perhaps because we care too much about the truth and not enough about people? Or because traditionally only our clergy preach and lead services? Frankly, I think that all such explanations are silly. What is much more likely is that we Lutherans are simply not convinced enough ourselves to go about convincing others. Consider car or sports enthusiasts. Do they need training in how to talk about their favorite models or teams, and endless exhortings to do so? No, they do it quite unselfconsciously, and to excess, because they enjoy and admire the objects of their loyalty, and are proud to identify with them.

"In other words, if Lutherans are to be contagious in their faith, they need to be convincing and therefore convinced as Lutherans—not as imitation Pentecostalists, imitation 'Evangelicals,' or imitation anything else. Such convictions cannot be 'put on,' as salesmanship bravado. They arise quite naturally, or I should say, supernaturally, from faithful preaching, faithful catechesis, faithful sacramental life, and faithful pastoral care—all upheld within the mutual solidarity of a faithful, confessionally sound congregation. Such a fount of conviction will draw others into the fold, the members' own life and confession being the chief 'cutting edge.'

"While the weekly Gospel proclamation will be the focal point of missionary attraction, compassion for the multitudes scattered like 'sheep having no shepherd' (St. Mt. 9:36) will hardly content itself with that. The Gospel can never accept ghetto-status within church-walls. Parochial schools are an ideal means for engaging the interest of families in the sacred riches of the Christian truth. Regular adult inquirers' classes ought to have their range of themes well publicized with the dignity befitting their subject-matter. Occasional public lectures may be given by the local pastor or by visiting missionaries or other specialists on pressing issues of Christian faith or life. And why not booths in shopping malls, publicizing such events, giving out free materials, and selling others, such as New Testaments, catechisms, hymnbooks, the Augsburg Confession, topical studies (but no religious junk-food)? The community would soon become aware that despite the zoo that is modern religion, there is a church which can be counted on to speak up for the historic Christian faith, with all due modesty and sobriety, but without flinching in the face of controversy. And shall we be shamed by Black Muslims and the impressive

Christian work of Chuck Colson, into reaching out to the tormented souls in our prisons?" (121-123).

"Mission Affirmations"

'There is no doubt that the Missouri Synod's 'Mission Affirmations' of 1965 reflect 'a new understanding of the mission of the church' (M. L. Kretzmann, 1965:114). While on leave from missionary service in India, Kretzmann had been appointed Mission Study Director, and his efforts culminated in the 'Mission Affirmations.' His anti-confessional outlook had become clear already in his (1957:7) attack on Sasse's sobering account of world Lutheranism's confessional crisis (1957:16-20)" (133).

Papal Infallibility and the CTCR

"Papal infallibility can appear, contrary to Acts 5:29, also in other churches in various guises, it seems that since 1992 the Missouri Synod, of all the unlikely churches, has a Theological Commission which is infallible when it speaks ex cathedra, that is in response to a request by a Dispute Resolution Panel for an opinion regarding 'a specific question of doctrine or doctrinal application.' In such cases, 'Any opinion received must be followed by the Dispute Resolution Panel' (Bylaw 8.21 i, 1992 Proceedings, p. 144)! Has anybody heard of Luther and Walther?" (136).

Hunter and Beautiful Diversity What Now?

"Hunter (1985b: 15-24) treats 'different denominations' as instances of a 'Beautiful Diversity' within 'The Body of Christ.' 'Churches differ because people are different,' we are told. But the denominations meant are all of a certain kind. A diagram of 'The Christian Church' pictures Trinity Lutheran Church, Grace Bible Church, Jonesville United Methodist Church, Fellowship Baptist Church, Mayville Church of Christ, and Faith Presbyterian Church simply as different 'shapes.' The Lutheran Church is here classified with non-sacramental and largely anti-confessional bodies, while the historic sacramental and liturgical churches do not appear at all! This little diagram speaks volumes about the sectarian self-image which links much modern Lutheranism with Schmucker. And it tallies with McGavran,1991, published under Hunter's editorship.

"Another Missouri Synod missiologist argues against confessional boundaries at the altar (J. Dretke, 1979:39-42) and holds that 'with all our different emphases, worship forms, and interpretations—Catholic, Protestant, Pentecostal, and new Spiritual church—we complement each other wonderfully well as we reach out to embrace God's world with His love (Rom. 12; 1 Cor. 12; 1 Pet .4:8-11)' (p. 192). Even more disturbing is Dretke's hesitation ('reserving judgment') to call Mohammed a 'false prophet' (pp. 83, 175). One would agree with this as an initial missionary accommodation, a subject on which Dretke has many valuable things to say. He rightly sees moral truth in Islam, for instance, and only as the sin-revealing 'light of the Law,' not the light of the Gospel (p. 225). But surely one cannot in principle keep the question of Mohammed's prophetic status open in one's preaching, teaching, and catechesis. Perhaps the basic trouble is an anti-doctrinal, personalist view of 'truth' (pp. 91-99; 137-139), not unlike that spear-headed by Emil Brunner in the heyday of neo-orthodoxy" (137-138).

What Now?

"Enough! 'Church Growth' is a mission paradigm shaped by a type of theology which as a whole does not square with the Lutheran understanding of the gospel. I chose four specific 'flashpoints' of conflict for detailed examination in this essay. The Gospel itself is at stake in all of them. That Gospel (including the sacraments) is alone pivotal, in Lutheran but not 'Church Growth' conviction, for conversion, for the ministry, for the church's worship, and for the orthodox confession and church" (139).

"Quite basic missionary intentions need to be clarified. What exactly do we seek in Russia, for instance? Assuming of course that we are there not to steal sheep but to convert unbelievers, do we seek to (a) edify individuals here and there, or (b) build an orthodox, confessional Lutheran church, or (c) simply meet needs within existing churches, thus helping to fasten the yoke of the Lutheran World Federation upon their necks, or (d) support pastors and congregations who, though at present belonging to doctrinally lax churches, earnestly desire to take a consistent stand for the Lutheran Confessions? Likewise in China, what are the implications of government-enforced pan-Protestant unionism? Is it possible at least to lay some foundations for a fully confessional church later?

"In Africa, it is true that our 'mission strategy reveals significant inconsistencies and perplexities when compared with the Lutheran Confessions' (Schulz, 1993:43-44)? The point at issue here is whether missionaries are to be pastors of churches, as is the practice of our German sister church's Bleckmar Mission, or whether they 'train leaders' and 'never serve one single congregation.' Which is more likely to build solid, confessional churches?" (140).

Changing LCMS Bylaws

"Is this a 'straw in the wind?' LCMS bylaws defining the role of circuit counselor were completely rewritten in 1989 'in the light of present-day needs.' The new version, in placing the counselor under the direction of the district president, does refer to 'doctrinal and spiritual supervision.' But the old 5.17 h, 'He shall inquire whether the congregations are zealously guarding the purity of doctrine, not tolerating errors or schismatic tendencies,' was dropped completely. Instead we have the new 5.13 c, 'Through his visitation to the congregations, he shall endeavor to strengthen the spirit of unity among congregations to effect mission and ministry and shall seek to strengthen and support the spirit of fellowship' (1989 Proceedings, p. 137). Nicer? More positive? Perhaps—and much more in tune with the 'upbeat,' see-no-evil, hear-no-evil, speak-no-evil mood of Church Growth.'

"If eye-brows are raised at occasional references to such mundane things as bylaws, as though that were 'church politics' rather than theology, the reminder is in order that its pragmatism makes 'Church Growth' a very political animal indeed. For example, an elaborate official pro-'Church Growth' production for an LCMS district in 1987 cited Lyle Schaller's suggestion of giving 'first priority' to organizing new congregations. One of the reasons was that 'in the organizations of new congregations, denominational leaders have a greater degree of control over what happens than in any other component of a denominational church growth strategy'!

"An antiseptically academic 'theology' disdaining all contact with actual church life is a pipe dream. The Lord's parables were the purest theology. But because they were pointedly concrete, church politicians resented them as intrusive (St. Lk. 20:19)" (141).

Church Membership Initiative and
The Great Commission Convocation

"Arguments of course must not be counted but weighed on the scales of the Scriptures and the Confessions. That means that endless survey-results, ringing the changes on 'change,' have little more than propaganda value. Take the Church Membership Initiative, lavishly funded by the Aid Association for Lutherans. The 'Narrative Summary of Fundings' and the 'Research Summary of Findings' (1993) reveal an approach both shallow and complacent. There is no interest at all in underlying theological maladies. But the project, a joint venture of the ELCA and the LCMS, with the Wisconsin Synod as observer, is not merely a fact-finding exercise, as is sometimes suggested. Its 'overall objective' is to set in motion forces that will result in annual increases in the number of members of Lutheran congregations.' Why would any confessional Lutheran wish to 'set in motion forces' for 'annual increases' in ELCA membership? The introductory page already alerts one to the hollowness of the talk about 'faithfulness to the substance of Lutheranism' (p. 3), by listing an ELCA official, a pastoress, as one of the sources of further information. 'Unchurched people feel good about their faith,' we are told, and the implication is that we should too.

'The summaries teem with predictable jargon and clichés. Despite the push for 'variety' of 'styles,' it is admitted that '[s]ome growing congregations offer only traditional forms of worship in a high quality manner.'

"Much of the *Church Membership Initiative* material is amplified and recycled in Loren Kramer (1994), which consists of 'compilations of 2,300 Partnership Sessions reports' from the Great Commission Convocation of 1993. Half of these respond to a video by 'researcher, Alan Klaas, consultant Cheryl Brown and director of evangelism Lyle Muller' of the *Church Membership Initiative*. Many of the sentiments cited are no doubt worthy, but the mere delivery, in statistical batches, of unargued snippets and sentences, on different sides of complex issues, is of doubtful value. Given the cultural presumption that whatever is, is right, views

125

graded only by statistics easily lend legitimacy and credibility to a theologically indefensible pluralism. Perhaps they can serve us as graphic reminders of the nature and extent of our church's confessional crisis, giving no rest to our consciences till that is faced and settled.

"Sticking our heads in the sand will not make the crisis go away. Quite the contrary. Failure to spot and resist hostile takeover spells the surrender of our Confession by default: 'Church growth is a process which, like yeast in dough, slowly but surely revolutionizes and reforms every segment of the church' (Hunter, 1983:29). The real secret of true and God-pleasing growth is plain evangelical, biblical, confessional integrity. Principle, therefore, not pragmatism, must settle the present free-for-all of church and mission paradigms. The noblest aim and prayer of theological work is that God's 'Word, as becomes it, may not be bound, but have free course and be preached to the joy and edifying of Christ's holy People'" (141-143).

AAL Funded Church Membership Initiative

"Among the notions I would not wish to legitimate by 'no fault' listings are the following: There needs to be some effective way to get to our seminaries so that our pastors can be prepared to lead people beyond pure doctrine stand. . .Christians should band together to do the Lord's work regardless of denomination . . . Accept paradigm shifts . . . Diversify services, create new ideas . . . develop a contemporary worship service . . . Re-think our position on "closed" communion . . . Surprised that [Church Membership Initiative] came from Synod and that leadership is waking up to change. . . Holy Communion should not be refused to a guest. . . seminaries need to be more careful to train future pastors to have a spirit of "openness"... Sense a tension in finding a balance. Tension between entertainment and worship'" (143).

Christian News, July 4, 1994

Marquart's Church Growth as Mission Paradigm – A Lutheran Assessment is a Lutheran Academy monograph published by Our Savior Lutheran Church, Houston, Texas.

Editor's notes:
* "On February 20, 2014, David Yonggi Cho, founder of Yoido Full Gospel Church in Seoul, long billed as the world's largest church, was sentenced to three years in prison for breach of trust and corruption." (*Christian News*, September 8, 2014, p. 15)

** Schuller's "Crystal Cathedral" has closed and is now a Roman Catholic church.

*** Since the Lutheran Church-Missouri Synod no longer disciplines tongues speaking healers, RIM has closed. Many of its leaders joined Jesus First, a group of liberals in the LCMS.

1. C. Peter Wagner, a leader of the Church Growth Movement concluded that somehow the techniques of the Church Growth Movement do not ____.
2. Wagner claimed the power to ____.
3. Wagner wrote the preface for a book by LCMS Church Growth leader ____.
4. The Roman Catholic Council of Trent strongly condemned ____.
5. Objective justification confesses both ____ and ____.
6. The Church Growth Movement bedazzles churches with ____.
7. Kent Hunter teaches that Church growth principles cause a church to ____.
8. Hunter refers to Pastor Kim as ____.
9. What did Synodical World Missions Director Scuderi produce? ____
10. Is everyone a minister? ____
11. What do LCMS charismatics fancy? ____
12. Where does the preaching and sacraments ministry instituted by Christ continue? ____
13. What did the Texas District's His Love, Our Response say about the gift of tongues? ____
14. What kind of church can be taken seriously? ____
15. The Lutheran World Federation urges ____.
16. It is high time for the church to stop trying to entertain the ____ and feed the ____.
17. ELCA stands for ____ and ____.
18. What is really racist? ____
19. What did Richard Resch say in "Hymnody Teacher of the Faith"? ____
20. Should simple hymns like "Just as I am" and "Rock of Ages" be used? ____
21. May Lutherans use "Amazing Grace"? ____
22. The church is not a museum for ____.
23. Lutherans have not convinced themselves to ____.
24. Lutherans need to be convinced as ____.
25. Parochial schools are an ideal means ____.
26. What about booths in shopping malls? ____
27. What should Lutherans do about tormented souls in prisons? ____
28. What did Herman Sasse say about M.L. Kretzmann's Mission Affirmations adopted by the LCMS? ____
29. Is the LCMS's CTCR infallible? ____
30. LCMS missiologist J. Dretke hesitated to call Mohammad ____.
31. What is likely to build more solid confessional churches in Africa and elsewhere? ____
32. What was dropped from LCMS bylaws? ____
33. The real secret of true and God pleasing church growth is ____.

A QUESTION OF FRAUD

No one will accuse The *Smalcald Articles* of pussyfooting. Yet our church there confesses that the "sublime articles" of the Trinity, the Incarnation, the Resurrection, and so on, "are not matters of dispute or contention" between the papal church and us, "for both parties confess them. Therefore, it is not necessary to treat them at greater length."

If this is no longer true, the fault is generally thought to lie with the Lutheran side. And so far as nominal world "Lutheranism" goes, the situation described by former Evangelical Church of Germany Chancery President Hans Asmussen is grim indeed, and has been for decades:

"But this is in fact the picture of wide sectors of our Lutheran Church today: clergymen read aloud the Christmas story, which they consider a fairy tale. They read aloud the Easter story, to which they find access only after several reinterpretations. At the grave, they witness to the resurrection of the dead, which they consider a myth" *(Lutheran World,* 1966, p. 186).

What is not generally realized is that the same abyss has meanwhile opened up within the Roman Catholic Church too. Writing in the *New York Review of Books* (June 14.1984), Loyola University (Chicago) Philosopher Thomas Sheehan described the reigning "liberal consensus:"

"In Roman Catholic seminaries...it is now common teaching that Jesus of Nazareth did not assert any of the messianic claims that the Gospels attribute to him and that he died without believing that he was Christ or the Son of God, not to mention the founder of a new religion.

"One would be hard pressed to find a [Roman] Catholic biblical scholar who maintains that Jesus thought he was the divine Son of God who preexisted from all eternity as the second person of the Trinity before he became a human being."

For such blunt speaking one would look in vain - a few courageous individuals aside—to the U.S. Roman Catholic bishops as a body, or to any other major church-political organ, for that matter. The "issue-managing" impulsive is to smother truth and honesty in a thick verbal full of "creative tensions," "pluralism," "culturally relevant re-interpretation," "dynamic unity in diversity," "counter-productive polarization," and similar secular claptrap. The point is that if the laity caught on, they would become alarmed, even angry, and that would not be good for business at all.

Yet bright laymen do catch on from time to time. And when they do, and speak their minds, apparatchiks wince at the unaccustomed candor, but devout souls everywhere are refreshed. If such a layman happens, moreover, to be the Wykeham Professor of Logic in the University of Oxford, it becomes difficult to denounce him as an overwrought bumpkin. Here are some of Prof. Michael Dummett's trenchant observations on the new "liberal consensus" in his (Roman Catholic) church, as published originally in the Dominican magazine *New Blackfriars*, and reprinted in the January 6, 1988 *News Weekly* of Australia:

"If the church is a fraud there can be no justification for belonging to it: no justification for complicity with fraud.

"Views like those commended by Sheehan might be combined with some religious belief in which Jesus played an important role, but not with anything recognizable as the Christian religion. If, in speaking of the Son of Man, Jesus was not referring to himself, then the Gospel accounts of his words are hopelessly garbled, and we cannot claim to know what he taught.

"If he did not believe himself divine, then we have no ground to do so, and hence commit idolatry in praying to him. If he knew nothing of the Trinity, then we know nothing of the Trinity, and have no warrant whatever for supposing that there is a Trinity.

"If he intended to found no community, then the church has no standing and is an imposter institution.

"It is easy to understand how someone may come to accept the views reported by Sheehan; it is straightforward case of loss of faith. Until very recently, those who suffered such a loss would, with pain, or a sense of liberation, or both, have separated themselves from the church...

"And, indeed, their actions are helping to transform the church into something distinctly fraudulent."

Where Do We Stand?

The Anglican Bishop of London, Dr. Graham Leonard, rightly says that all major Christian churches today are rent by a deep internal schism between traditional believers and the liberals. The later hold the "both Scripture and tradition have lost their authority," and want "to reshape Christianity in accordance with modern ideas."

Why is not more heard about this from leading Lutheran church-men? In North American Lutheranism the schism has become institutionalized, the ELCA representing, at least at the professional level, the "liberal consensus" of historical criticism, while the Missouri Synod and some smaller bodies stand for "Old Lutheranism." Since our Synod has had its own bout at historical criticism, and deliberately expelled that spirit eagerly embraced by others, one would have thought that "Missouri" is now in an excellent position to raise the alarm with clear, loud, and long trumpet blasts (I Cor. 14:8). Instead, our official Synod posture is often strangely half-hearted. We face total sellout of the faith, and waffle diplomatically as if it were a matter of "nuance" and "fine-tuning."

Take that Puerto Rico conference last year, sponsored jointly by the Lutheran World Federation's Ecumenical Institute in Strasbourg, and the expiring Lutheran Council in the U.S.A. The theme was, "Basic Consensus—Basic Differences." The slogan would have summed up the situation nicely—four and a half centuries ago at Smalcald! But what "basic consensus" can there be with those who surrender the "sublime articles" of the Trinity and the Incarnation? The conference included "representatives of the Lutheran, Orthodox, Catholic, Reformed, and Anglican traditions." Did the matter of the deep rift in all those church even come up? The ecumenical managers who must keep their broken Humpty-

Dumpties together artificially, do not mind at all admitting "differences"—so long as there is a still more fundamental "basic consensus" to appeal to. Who, apart from these politicians, is really served by the polite pretenses? Certainly not the rank-and-file Christians in the various churches.

The LCUSA Statement on Historical Criticism (1986) suffered from the same malady. The introduction expressly refers to the Missouri Synod's 1981 request to the Division of Theological Studies to consider "the far-reaching implications of historical criticism, as practiced in U.S. Lutheranism," for "the central, Christological-Trinitarian core of the Gospel." It also states: "Time has not permitted us to do this" (!). Then follow "Points of Agreement" and "Points of Disagreement" about historical criticism. Finally, "A Word to the Churches" assures all and sundry that the "sharp disagreement" recognized in some "areas" nevertheless "did not destroy our sense of oneness in Christ."

Granted that all those in whom the Holy Spirit has through Word and Sacraments created faith, are one in Christ—although that oneness remains hidden in this age (Col. 3:3). We can grasp it with assurance only in the church's pure marks, the pure Gospel and Sacraments of Christ. Granted also that the historic Christian confessions, Eastern Orthodox, Roman Catholic, Lutheran, and Reformed (including Anglican), shared a common foundation in the Trinitarian dogma. But the deep rift in all these churches has radically changed all that. When the ELCA's leading dogmatics book, *Christian Dogmatics*, shamelessly ridicules Christ's divine nature as "Jesus' metaphysical double" and as an "extra entit[y]," and interprets away the Holy Trinity (I, 154-155), official statements may not speak of "our oneness in Christ." Christ and the critical Belial have nothing in common (II Cor. 6:15). Silence here is "complicity with fraud."

Can our Synod learn again to speak as honestly and responsibly as do an Anglican bishop and a Roman Catholic professor of logic?

Prof. Kurt Marquart
Concordia Theological Seminary
Fort Wayne, Indiana

From AFFIRM, June, 1988.
Christian News, July 13, 1988

1. How did Hans Asmussen describe nominal world Lutheranism? ____
2. What did Roman Catholic Thomas Sheehan say about Roman Catholic seminaries? ____
3. The "issue-managing" impulsive is to ____.
4. If the church is a fraud there is no justification for ____.
5. If Jesus knew nothing of the Trinity then ____
6. What did Bishop Leonard Graham say about all major Christian churches? ___
7. How does the LCMS face total sellout of the faith? ____
8. ELCA's leading dogmatics book *Christian Dogmatics* shamelessly ridicules ____.

THE CASE FOR FULL-TIME CHRISTIAN EDUCATION

Excerpts from an address the editor delivered at the annual banquet of The Association for Christian Schools in the Shamrock Hilton Hotel, Houston, Texas, April 13, 1967. Much of the material in parts IV and V of this speech are from an unpublished essay by Kurt Marquart.

* * *

IV. CHRISTIAN SCHOOLING IS FOR THE WHOLE OF LIFE

One's work in life (whether as pastor, farmer, housewife, laborer, businessman, or any other useful occupation), and proper preparation for it, are important, indeed sacred, for Holy Scripture says: "let him labor, working with his hands the thing which is good, that he may have to give to him that needeth" (Ephesians 4:28), Christian schooling, regarding work as a sacred service rather than a mere necessary evil, will therefore be even more conscientious about preparing boys and girls for their earthly careers, than are secular institutions.[47]

The Christian educator, however, knows that man was not made merely to work, suffer, and play here on earth for a few years, and then to disappear into the grave forever. In Christ God has provided a happy and useful future for men, which will have no end. If this is true, if men and women were really created by God to glorify Him and enjoy His loving companionship, if they were really redeemed—after the Fall—from sin and death by His own blood, and if they are really sanctified by His own Spirit, through Word and Sacrament, many important things follow; for example:

A. Nothing is more important then reaching this wonderful, eternal destiny. "Again, the kingdom of heaven is like unto treasure hid in a field; the which when a man hath found, he hideth, and for joy thereof goeth and selleth all that he hath, and buyeth that field. Again, the kingdom of heaven is like unto a merchant man, seeking goodly pearls; who, when he had found one pearl of great price, went and sold all that he had, and bought it" (Matt. 13:44-46). "Seek ye first the Kingdom of God and His righteousness, and all these things shall be added unto you!" (Matt. 6:33).

B. Schooling which prepares only for this earthly life, but denies, questions, or ignores God, His Word, and the life to come is not worthy of the name. It is that most dangerous of all lies: a half-truth! Jesus said; "For what is a man profited, if he shall gain the whole world, and lose his own soul? or what shall a man give in exchange for his soul" (Matt. 16:26).

C. The Word of God must not be added mechanically to other points of view and facts; rather, it must rule, permeate, illuminate, and unify everything else. This means that ALL of life, all work and knowledge, must submit to God's Word. Christianity is not a "Sunday-religion": It claims our whole lives. "Thou shalt love the Lord, thy God with ALL thy

131

heart, and with ALL thy soul, and with ALL thy mind" (Matt. 22:37). "Casting down imaginations, and every high thing that exalteth itself against the knowledge of God, and bringing into subjection EVERY thought to the obedience of Christ" (2 Cor. 10:5).

D. Parents have no more solemn duty to their children than to give them a truly Christian education. "These words which I command thee this day shall be in thine heart; and thou shalt teach them DILIGENTLY unto thy children" (Deut. 6:6,7). "Train up a child in the way he should go, and when he is old he will not depart from it" (Prov. 22:6). "And ye fathers, provoke not your children to wrath: but bring them up in the nurture and admonition of the Lord" (Eph. 6:4). "And that from a child thou hast known the holy scriptures, which are able to make thee wise unto salvation, through faith which is in Christ Jesus. . ." (2 Tim. 3:15).

E. Christian education is for everyone, young and old, but it is particularly essential in connection with formal schooling. "As newborn babes, desire the sinceire milk of the word, that ye may grow thereby" (1 Peter 2:2).

F. Not only parents, but the whole Church as such, AND THERE-FORE ALL MEMBERS OF IT, are responsible for Christian schooling, particularly of the little ones: "Feed my lambs" (John 21:15). "Suffer the little children to come unto Me, and forbid them not, for of such is the Kingdom of God" (Mark 10:14). "Go and make disciples of all people: Baptize them into the name of the Father, the Son, and the Holy Spirit, and teach them to do everything I have commanded you" (Matthew 28:19, 20).

G. Earthly kingdoms and states, recognizing the necessity of education for the welfare of the state itself, oblige not only parents but ALL citizens to maintain the schools. Christians belong to the most wonderful Kingdom and Commonwealth of all, and therefore gladly assume the responsibility to build one another in faith and love. (1 Cor. 12:12 ff.; Eph. 2:19 ff.)

V. WHY FULL-TIME CHRISTIAN SCHOOLS?

Please note first of all that when we advocate full-time Christian schooling we do NOT mean;

*That part-time agencies, like Sunday Schools, are unimportant;

*That public-school children cannot be saved, or cannot grow up to be good Christians;

*That all graduates of Christian schools are always good Christians, or at least better than graduates of public schools (There was a Judas even among the Twelve Apostles);[48]

*That public school teachers, as individuals, are godless;

*That Christian youth should never be exposed to atheistic philosophies and anti-Christian theories;

*That Christian youth are not going to have to live in a world of sin and evil.[49]

Some Advantages of Full-Time Christian Schooling

It is clear that only a full-time, consciously Christian school can do justice to the demands of a truly complete, well-rounded Christian education. Consider some of the obvious advantages of the Christian school:

1. Regular, daily devotions, and corporate participation in Church life.

2. Thorough instruction in God's truth—daily lessons. God's Word is not like a pagan charm or prayer-wheel. It does not work magically or automatically. Since its power lies not in its sound but in its sense, it must be understood, studied, pondered, applied. Casual, hit and miss instruction can't do that. Daily systematic study of it is ideal.

3. Christian discipline, fellowship, friendship.

The Fundamental Advantage of Full-Time Christian Schooling

Many think that the above three points constitute the real benefit of Full-Time Christian schooling. It is true that these benefits alone are very precious, and alone justify the existence of Christian schools. THE FUNDAMENTAL SIGNIFICANCE OF CHRISTIAN SCHOOLS, HOWEVER, LIES NOT IN A PROCESS OF SIMPLE ADDITION (EDUCATION PLUS RELIGION), BUT, AS IT WERE, IN ONE OF MULTIPLICATION (EDUCATION SHAPED BY RELIGION)! It is this fundamental fact above all that must be clearly grasped.

The Christian school does not simply add religion to the ordinary curriculum, but teaches EVERY subject in the light of God's Word. This means that the child is being given a COMPLETE education, and a right, whole, and wholesome view of reality and life. The child's mind is not artificially split into a "secular" and a "religious" compartment. Rather, the child's outlook, shaped and unified by the Word of God, is solid, meaningful, and practical.

The Principal of Concordia Memorial College, Toowoomba, (Queensland, Australia), has rightly said in an essay on Christian Education:

> No education is a true education which does not view man in the completeness of his humanity, body and soul, and in the light of his twofold existence, temporal and eternal.
>
> Any education, no matter how extensive and profound is incomplete and distorted and ultimately futile if it fails to recognize the basic importance of the nature of man in relation to his Creator and in the light of his eternal destiny.
>
> The question for us is: What is the best for the Kingdom of God? The answer is complete Christian education for the sake of the individual and the State as well as the Church.
>
> It is a delusion to think that the school meets the requirements of the Christian Church by the mere fact that "religious instruction" is given as a subject. On the contrary, the Christian church demands a school in which not only a correct pedagogy is maintained but also the total life of the school, as well as the instruction in all the subjects, is (shaped) by the Gospel. AN EDUCATION THAT

133

AVOIDS ALL REFERENCE TO GOD AND HIS PLACE IN THE WORLD BY THAT VERY FACT FOSTERS A GODLESS WORLD VIEW, NAMELY IN SO FAR AS IT ACCUSTOMS THE CHILDREN TO LEAVE GOD OUT OF ACCOUNT IN THEIR THINKING.

Religious training should keep pace with secular intellectual training or the whole development of the individual is thrown out of balance. We must repudiate the reasoning which says that the State is responsible for the child's general education, the home and the Church for his religious education. Our church cannot approve of a general education from which religion is absent, for education without religion is incomplete education.[50]

Time and Atmosphere

Modern educators are keenly aware of the fact that some of the most effective influences on the child are the unspoken assumptions, the atmosphere of the schooling, working indirectly and informally, but powerfully to establish basic beliefs, attitudes, habit-patterns. The very fact of time spent on various subjects is significant: If a child sees that temporal education is provided compulsorily and efficiently for five days a week, seven hours a day, but that religious instruction is a voluntary hour or two per week, this very fact works subconsciously in his mind to establish the conclusion that temporal learning is vital, important, necessary, and "real," whereas "religion" is an additional element which some people may choose, but without which most people get along quite well, educationally.

You Ask Me Why

"You Ask Me Why," a tract available from the Association for Christian Schools, well summarizes the case for full time Christian schooling:

You ask me why I send my children to the Christian school?

Well, now that's a good question. I know what you're thinking. The public schools have just as good facilities and teachers as the Christian schools, and sometimes even better. So why all this fuss and bother of setting up a separate school system? Why not teach the children religion at home or in church or Sunday school?

But, you see, you've asked me something that gets right to the core of the meaning of life. If Christian schools meant simply tacking on a prayer each day, or an extra course in Bible study, they wouldn't be worth all the time and expense.

I send my children to the Christian school because I believe that ALL of life is religious, God is at the center of everything. He made all things. He guides and controls them, and He demands that we, His creatures, honor Him as Lord and Savior in everything we do.

Of course that includes our studying, as well as our everyday work. It includes every part of life, without exception. It means that I can't be satisfied with submitting my children to Christian training at home and church only. As a parent, I'm responsible for those thirty important hours that they spend each week in school. Some of the most significant training of my children takes place in the school atmosphere. How can I leave God out of the picture here?

But, you say, what's the difference if my child studies arithmetic, history, or literature in a public school or in a Christian school?

Much, I want my child to learn, from his earliest years, that all of life belongs to God and was made for Him.

-In science, I want him to know that he is studying God's laws for the universe.

-In history, I want him to see the unfolding of God's plan for the ages and the redemption of His people.

-In literature, I want him to test other writers by Christian standards so that he will appreciate what is good and true and beautiful, and discern what is false or dishonoring to God.

-In civics, I want him to know that true government is ordained of God and requires our loyalty and support. I want him to learn the principles of honesty, decency, co-operation, and fair play because these are rules that God has set up for the ordering of our life together.

-All this is a big order. It can't be accomplished in fifteen or thirty minutes a day. It takes everything we've got to instill in the hearts of our children that true fear of the Lord which is "the beginning of all wisdom."

Moses said it thousands of years ago. He told the people of Israel then how to bring up their children—God's covenant children. This is how he said it: "Therefore shall ye lay up these words in your heart and in your soul, and bind them for a sign upon your hand, that they may be as frontlets between your eyes. And ye shall teach them when thou sittest in thine house, and when thou walkest by the way, when thou liest down, and when thou risest up. And thou shalt write them upon the door posts of thine house, and upon thy gates. (Deut, 11:18-20)

This means Christian education—in all of life.

Expensive? Yes, of course. We pay our full share of taxes for the public schools, and we support our Christian schools in addition to this.

But we count it a privilege to have this wonderful opportunity, in a land of freedom, to dedicate ourselves and our children entirely to God.

Would you like to know more about our Christian schools, how they are operated, supported, what policies and curricula prevail? You are invited to write or call your local Christian school.

Evolutionary Development

It should also be said that State education will be increasingly secular, materialistic, evolutionistic, naturalistic. The fundamental assumption is becoming more brazenly evident that man is but an accidental, evolutionary development of an impersonal universe consisting only of matter (or energy!) in motion.[51] God, His power. His influence. His Will, His

135

work, and His Word, may be mentioned, if at all, then only in the vaguest and most general terms—anything else would be "sectarian"! In the teaching of history, Christianity and the Church are not given their proper due. "Science" and "Social concerns" have become sacred cows. References to religion and to the supernatural are often associated with legends, humor, and primitive superstition.

The fact is that certain facts do not speak for themselves. They must be seen in some light, some perspective. They are understood either in the light of God and His Creation, or understood in the darkness of the evolutionary superstition: self-development out of chaos. On the question of God in education, one cannot be neutral; Not to mention Him is to deny Him, as He said: "He that is not with Me is against Me!" The Christian school, on the other hand, accepting God, the Creator of "ALL things, visible AND INVISIBLE," is free to educate truly and fully:

1. It develops the WHOLE child, body, mind, soul, spirit.

2. It has shown itself to be capable of teaching basic academic subjects successfully. Graduates of Christian schools have entered hundreds of professions and callings,

3. It provides steady motivation and training that the child may be an informed and eager witness and worker for Christ.

4. It teaches "in view of eternity." It teaches that men are not to disappear into the grave forever. It is free to teach the Christian faith fully and specifically, as taught in God's Word.[52]

5. It does not merely add "religion" to "secular" subjects. God and His Word are central and pervade the teaching of all subjects.

6. Day after day the Christian faith, heritage, and life are constant influences on the child's mind and personality.

7. Both students and teachers live and work daily at the foot of the Cross,

8. It teaches loyalty to Church and State, and develops a growing appreciation of Christian culture as expressed in art, music, literature, etc.

Conclusion

Government schooling is becoming increasingly evolutionistic and materialistic. Its religious and philosophical foundations are not Christian. Government schools are not neutral towards religion. They do teach a religion, secular humanism, which is hostile towards historic Christianity.

Religion courses and "the objective teaching about religion" are not an adequate substitute for full-time Christian schooling. Historic Christianity and the Holy Scriptures are attacked in many of these courses, even in religion courses taught in church-related colleges.

Christian schooling prepares boys and girls for their earthly careers and for a happy and useful future, which will have no end. Only a full-time, consciously Christian school can do justice to the demands of a truly complete Christian education. There is a CASE FOR FULL-TIME CHRISTIAN SCHOOLING.

Footnotes

[49] Bob Jones Jr., President of Bob Jones University, Greenville, SC, answers those who argue that full-time Christian schooling does not properly prepare youth to live in a world of sin and evil:

It has always been a source of great wonder to me that some supposedly mature and intellectual Christians...should advise young people to attend a secular school. "After all, you are a Christian, you are going to have to face a world that is godless and unchristian. You will not develop in your spiritual resistance if you are sheltered and protected from atheistic philosophies and from the contact with intellectual rationalism: and, of course, you will be more respected by scholarly men and women. Besides, Christian colleges have low academic standards and inadequate equipment." Let's look at the fallacies in these high-sounding words.

Of course, young people are going to have to live in a world of sin and evil. They cannot always be protected from temptations, moral and intellectual, but they should not be exposed to such temptations until they have been well-grounded and inoculated against them. Can you imagine a man saying, "My son will, no doubt, be exposed to typhoid fever and smallpox in life; therefore I am going to expose him now while he is young, so he will build up a resistance."

In the first place, that is not the way to build up a resistance. In the second place, even if it were, only a crazy man would so expose a child when he could have him inoculated. In other words, why risk the child's becoming infected with resultant illness and possible death when inoculation and vaccination can provide immunity?

Immunity against loss of faith, against sin and immorality can be acquired during college years, but not by exposure to these things on the campus and in the classrooms of a godless institution. Rather, resistance is built by being well-grounded in faith and the Word of God in a Christian institution.

Jones further states:

Second: A Christian college does NOT try to keep its students in ignorance of the philosophies and theories now popular in our day, but which are contrary to the Word of God. A Christian Institution simply does not try to "sell" these theories and philosophies to its students as factual and true. Rather it tests them by the Word of God and shows them up for what they are unscriptural philosophies and hypotheses unproved and unsound.

Every once in a while someone says, "Of course, you don't teach evolution in Bob Jones University." Certainly, we teach evolution in Bob Jones University! But we teach evolution as a theory, which is invalid in the light of the Word of God. We want our students to know what Darwin taught. They read his ORIGIN OF THE SPECIES.

Investigation will prove that the Christian colleges of America, large or small, are well prepared as regards faculty training, buildings and equipment for the courses which they offer. Certain advanced technical and scientific courses may not be available in all Christian institutions because the demand for such courses is small in proportion to the expensive equipment necessary.

[50] Quoted in an unpublished essay by Kurt Marquart, Toowoomba, Australia. Much of the material in parts IV and V of this speech is from this unpublished essay by Marquart titled "The Case For Full-Time Christian Education."

[51] "Two Billion Years Of Evolution," the cover story in the January 15, 1967 ST. LOUIS GLOBE-DEMOCRAT SUNDAY MAGAZINE, includes pictures of school children gazing at exhibits in the "Hall of Evolution" in the St. Louis Museum of Science and Natural History. The story says in part:

The evolution of life is a long and complex story told in fossils, bones

137

and concepts. It spans over 2 billion years and hangs on facts and theories that keep right on increasing.

Small wonder, then, that big museums display acres of fossil evidence and miles of description to trace the development of life on earth from amoeba to fish, to amphibians, to reptiles, to mammals and men.

But it is quite a feat when a small museum, with limited space and very few bones and fossils, can capsule the whole evolution theory and make it "come through" in a fresh, clear way.

The St. Louis Museum of Science and Natural History has done it... But when the museum had no bones or fossils to illustrate some point (to compare 'a lobed fin with an amphibian leg, for example) the museum staff simply molded them in plaster and they came out looking just like the real thing...

Today, school children are regular visitors at the evolution exhibit in the St. Louis Museum of Science and Natural History. After all, 1967 is a long way from 1925. But it's only a moment in the story of life that goes back two billion years.

[52] Christian schools should consider including Greek and Hebrew in their curriculums for advanced students. The best methods of modern language studies could be used in order that these students may be able to study the Holy Scriptures in the original languages.

1. Christian schooling is for the ____ of life.
2. Nothing is more important than ____.
3. All of life, all work, and knowledge must submit to ____.
4. Parents have no more solemn duty to their children than to give them

   ____.
5. What are some advantages of Christian schools? ____
6. What is the fundamental advantage of full-time Christian schooling?

   ____
7. Should a child's mind be split into a "secular" and "religious" department?____
8. Education without religion is ____.
9. State education will be increasingly ____.

WHY NOT EFFECTIVE PARENTAL
CHOICE OF SCHOOLS?

"End of the Line for VOUCHERS," triumphantly proclaims the June 1976 issue of *Church & State,* official organ of Americans United for Separation of Church and State. People as diverse as economists Milton Friedman (conservative) and Christopher Jencks (liberal) have welcomed the voucher plan. It is obviously designed to maximize genuine educational freedom and pluralism.

Under this plan parents of all school-children would, in *Church & State's* own words, receive tax-funded vouchers "equivalent in value to the average amount normally spent per student per year in public schools," which would then "be used by parents to pay tuition to the public, parochial, or private school of their choice."

It is difficult to imagine a scheme more ideally suited to the interests of real justice in a modern, pluralist society. One of the very cornerstones of our civilization is the principle recognized in Article 26 of the *Universal Declaration of Human Rights:* "Parents have a prior right to choose the kind of education that shall be given to their children." It is all very well to say that people are free to send their children to religious or other private schools if they wish. If the cost of such private education is prohibitive, the average person has no chance to exercise this "right." It becomes, in effect, a privilege of a well-to-do elite. Other citizens simply have to put up with the secular, amoral, evolutionist/humanistic indoctrination which increasingly shapes government dispensed "education" in the Western world. Moreover, Christian parents, who may abhor the secularist educational monopoly, are compelled to support it with their tax-money — and are considered insolent meddlers if they dare to object to the more blatant anti-Christian propaganda in textbooks!

Clearly, the voucher scheme is a most effective remedy. It is perfectly fair that parents/taxpayers should have access on equal terms to public funds for the schools of their own choice. One may on various grounds deplore *any* Federal involvement in education. But that is now an academic question. Given the fact that Federal funds are being appropriated, no school can in the long term remain viable unless it has access either to public funds or to private wealth. And the church has no business running "snob schools" for a select few. Yet *Church & State* denounces the eminently sensible voucher proposal in the most hysterical terms. For example, the scheme is held to "reduce pluralism and variety in education by providing public subsidies for religious and ideological homogenization within voucher schools. . ."!

One would have thought that it is precisely pluralism and variety that would benefit from the plan. The trouble is that the people who talk most about pluralism really mean by it not a genuine plurality of views, but one single secularist perspective, filled with a homogenized mishmash of relativized views, and imposed on the public through one standard system of government schools. This kind of bogus "pluralism" has, of course, every reason to fear vouchers, for they would effectively take the power of choice away from the educational bureaucrats and restore it to those to whom it rightfully belongs, the parents. If "pluralism" is the name of the game, then let us play it with an honest deck. Even the Supreme Court (*Torcaso v. Watkins,* 1961) has defined "secular humanism" as a religion entitled to protection under the First Amendment. Neither traditional phobias and jealousies nor genuine confessional differences among Christians ought to blind us to the fact that in the name of the First Amendment the nominal Christian majority in this country are being educationally disfranchised by a secular humanist minority.

Oddly enough, *Church & State* also attacks vouchers for the opposite reason: they "provide public subsidy for dividing children and teachers by religion, race, ideology, class and in other ways, *thereby weakening interfaith and community harmony. . .*" (my emphases). So we really lack the stomach for pluralism after all! Is American nationhood so fragile and precarious that it needs education for cultural conformity to keep it from shattering? One is reminded of Hitler's suffocating slogan: "One People, One Reich, One Fuehrer"! Surely our Bicentennial celebrates something more substantial!

Not surprisingly, the voucher idea has attracted favorable attention overseas. The 1974 "Statement of Principles" of the National Council of Independent Schools (Australia) strongly argues the need for access to public funds if parental choice of education is to be meaningful. The document explicitly refers to "some form of voucher or warrant" as one acceptable "mechanism for recurrent grants." And the Australian publication *News Weekly* (March 10, 1976) expresses great interest in the voucher experiment in the Alum Rock, California, school district. The paper reports:

58% of the teachers thought that, in general, the voucher demonstration would increase the quality of education received by the children of Alum Rock, while 8% thought quality would decrease. . . .

On the issue of quality of parents' choices, 93% of the teachers rated these choices as good or fair. In addition, 62% of the voucher teachers thought actual classroom innovation had increased, while only 9% were of the opposite opinion.

Is it not high time to end the monopolization of the First Amendment by the secular humanists?

Additional material is available from Citizens for Educational Freedom, 844 Washington Building, Washington D.C. 20005.

Christian News, September 19, 1977

1. What is the voucher plan? ____
2. What increasingly shapes government dispensed education in the western world? ____
3. The power of choice belongs to ____.
4. The Supreme Court defined secular humanism as ____.

INDEX

142

www.ingramcontent.com/pod-product-compliance
Lightning Source LLC
Chambersburg PA
CBHW071858090426
42811CB00004B/663